Dear Samuel

—A NOVEL—

Barry Ivker

ISBN 978-1-950818-72-3 (paperback)

Rushmore Press LLC
1 888 733 9607
www.rushmorepress.com

Barry Ivker
2559 Foothills Drive
Hoover, AL 35226
e-mail: drfbi1@gmail.com

Printed in the United States of America

A native of Birmingham, AL exiles himself from his hometown. His father is a member of the KKK, his mother died giving birth to him, and he is saddened/sickened by the violence associated with the Civil Rights struggle. He supports himself by selling Romanian rugs (imitation of Persian rugs at a third of the price) and sex toys. The whole novel is in the form of letters he writes to a friend who collects first day of issue envelopes/stamps. The exile continues until 1971, when, as the title indicates, he returns to Birmingham somewhat the worse for wear.

DEAR SAMUEL: Wherein it is recorded the remarkable peregrination of Dwayne ____________, who exiled himself from his native town for twelve years and returned home somewhat the worse for wear.

For Rev. Fred Shuttlesworth and the Staff of the Civil Rights Institute of Birmingham, Alabama.

PREFACE

One of the things I most enjoy doing is going to estate sales. Call it the excitement of the hunt—the prospects of finding a book by an author I had not known before, an artifact from some exotic culture, or even some dishes with a pattern I remembered from childhood. There is always the mystique of trying to reconstruct the life of someone who has died—seeing the things they valued spread out, to be snatched up by anyone willing to pay the asking price, much as my things will be dispersed when I am gone.

There is always the prospect of finding something totally unexpected. Thus it was some months ago when I came across a box of envelopes all marked First Day of Issue. The United States Postal Service designates a city on the first day a given stamp is issued, and all letters mailed from that city on that day can be cancelled with that marking. Frequently, dealers get bundles of such cancelled envelopes and sell them to collectors for a good price.

Here was a boxful of these envelopes. I offered the sellers a price for the whole box. It was near the end of the sale. The sellers wanted to get rid of as much as possible, and they accepted my offer.

I should add that I am not a stamp collector. I do have friends who collect stamps and thought this would make a nice gift for one of them.

When I got home, I arranged the collection chronologically. They spanned a period of twelve years, from 1959 to 1971. They were all addressed to the same person in Birmingham, Alabama, a Samuel __________. They were all written by the same person, a Dwayne ________, who was born and raised in Birmingham. My curiosity was piqued.

Who was this son of Birmingham who absented himself from his native town during one of the most turbulent periods of its history? What was the relationship of the two men that warranted such a long and voluminous correspondence—for me, a one-way correspondence, since I had no way of retrieving the letters Samuel sent to Dwayne.

Why the long period of exile during that particular period of time? Why the widespread traveling? How did Dwayne manage to support himself? What did he do to occupy his time? My mind was filled with questions. When I started reading the letters, the answers I received were far more intriguing than I could have imagined.

It is with this in mind that I offer this correspondence to the reading public. It reflects the psychological history not only of an unusual personality but also of an important era of American history.

I have let the letters stand as they were written, preserving the style, grammar, and orthography of the author. I know little enough of the details of his childhood. He was obviously well read, even if he was not formally educated to any advanced degree. He was clearly an astute observer of the events of his time.

It is my hope that the reader will find the letters edifying and entertaining—useful and pleasing—and that my effort to bring them to public view will be deemed worthwhile.

B. Ivker
2010

March 30, 1959

Dear Samuel,

New York City. I've been here for over a week. Establishing contacts. Business before pleasure. I've made the contacts. All is going well in that regard. Time for a little sightseeing.

As the envelope indicates, I'm at the United Nations Building. You told me it was time to see a bit of the world. Well, the world is here. Everybody, it seems, comes to New York and not just to the UN. I was walking through a market area on the Lower East Side. Packed with people, some in exotic garb. Talking languages I couldn't even recognize. And the locals—every different shade. That took some getting used to. Blacks and whites together in shops, on buses and subways, in restaurants. Nobody seemed to care one way or the other. The only thing that was important was getting a bargain, outselling competitors, getting somewhere, or getting a meal. Salesmen shouting or even singing their wares and their prices to passersby. Arguing with customers about prices. People rushing by so fast—barely noticing each other. The bargaining is almost always a shouting match—as if a fight were about to break out, but it never does. People insulting each other over a pair of socks and then moving on as if nothing had happened.

I made the contacts you told me about, Romanians. I saw what they had to offer. Carpets that look Oriental in design and manufacture but crafted in Romania at a fraction of the cost of the originals. I think there's a good market for carpets like this. A good profit margin selling to upscale outlets, especially in the Northeast and Midwest. I met with Danish sales representatives, but I don't think you want to know about that. Can't put all of one's eggs in one basket. A somewhat higher risk dealing with their merchandise. Potential confiscations and prosecutions, but I'll be careful about transport and who I show the merchandise to.

Notice the postmark on the envelope. "First day of issue." You can only get that by mailing a letter from the UN Post Office on the day the stamp is issued. I thought you'd like that. I know you collect

American stamps. Plate blocks. This might be something new for you. Apparently the U.S. Postal Service does the same thing with American stamps. It designates one city and a date of issue. I'm not sure how collectors get to all the cities to fill out this collection, but the central Post Office gave me a list of the cities and the dates. I'll be traveling around selling my merchandise, so I might be able to get you a few more "First Day" covers. They make it nice. Give you a fancy envelope to go along with the stamp. I'll see what I can do. This issue comes in four- and eight-cent denominations. For the eight-cent stamp, I must mail you an envelope. They let you do that. Tomorrow they issue a four-cent stamp commemorating the Tenth Anniversary of NATO. I'm not sure what NATO is all about, but they give you information sheets to go along with the envelopes, so I guess I'll find out. It's no big deal to go to the UN building. It's not far from some of the business outlets I plan to visit. The only problem is parking. A lot of money just to get a commemorative envelope with a four-cent stamp on it. But if you are interested in collecting these envelopes, it's the least that I can do. And the UN building is really beautiful. Nothing like it back home. And all those flags out front. I do a guessing game and try to figure out which flag goes with which country. Some of these countries I never heard of. We didn't study much geography when I was in school. I couldn't even identify all the states in our country. If you asked me to find Kansas or Wisconsin, I might have a problem there. I'm not sure I could tell the difference between Vermont and New Hampshire. Maybe I'll get up that way and find out.

By the way, I'll be getting a Post Office box, so you can write to me. Send me news from the home front. I've only been gone for a week, but I'm already missing down-home cooking. You can find French restaurants here—German, Italian, Greek, Turkish, and whatnot. I haven't found a single place yet where I can get some good grits. Seven days. Not a single person has said, "Bless your heart."

April 1, 1959

Dear Samuel,

Moving around the city. Anything goes here. I saw a man walking around on the Avenue of the Americas dressed in Viking clothing. Just walking back and forth like he was on some kind of scouting mission. I asked a few people who he was. They shrugged their shoulders and said, "He's the Viking," like it was the most normal thing in the world to see someone dressed like that, parading back and forth in the middle of the city. And that was only the beginning. You see couples—black and white, two men, two women. You can imagine what would happen back home. Here it passes for normal. I think you could have them walking stark naked on Fifth Avenue, and no one would give it a second thought.

I went to a jazz club last night—in Harlem. Back home they would have called it nigger music. My father would have called it nigger music. The kind of stuff no good churchgoer would listen to. The crowd was really into it. A mixed crowd. Bull would have had a fit. A bunch of degenerate Commies, he would say. But some of the crowd were dressed like real gentlemen and ladies—as if they were going to the opera. And some were dressed outlandishly. Some looked like they just got out of the gutter. They were all mixed up—like it was nothing special for a woman in an evening gown to be right next to a guy with earrings and hair like it hadn't been combed or washed in months. All people cared about was grooving to the music. Grooving. That's what they say. And booze was flowing like water. The smoke was thick enough to cut with a knife. I was dressed down a bit. No use calling attention to myself in a neighborhood like this. I made it a point to leave with some others so I wouldn't be walking alone at one o'clock in the morning. Why take chances? But the music was good. Really good. And it wasn't going to come to me in my boarding house. You have to take some chances in this world.

I got tickets to see some major league baseball. You know how much I like to see a good game. The Dodgers are here. The Yankees too. They got blacks and whites playing on the same team. Blacks and whites all mixed together in the stands. It's like I'm in another country.

I made some contacts to sell my rugs. Good profit margin. With the other stuff too. They call them adult shops here. If anyone would dare to open a shop like that back home, they would be shut down in a minute. No telling who would get there first, the police or the temperance ladies. And it's not just seedy-looking types that are buying. Men dressed in pin-striped suits, like they were just taking off a few minutes from their banking jobs to leaf through some girlie magazines—to buy some stuff to spice up their lives in their suburban bedrooms. A real den of iniquity. Sin city. But like I said, everything goes here. Everybody takes it for being normal.

You see the stamps. N.A.T.O. An international organization of European countries and the U.S. to hold the Commies in check. Old Bull would take one look at this city and say that the Commies are already running wild here—that the battle was already lost.

I'm going to be hitting the road tomorrow—looking to market wares in some smaller towns—to get to see more of this great country of ours. Get a better perspective on things. Isn't that what you told me way back when? Travel broadens your mind. Hey, I even found a place that serves grits. Not as good as back home, but it was something.

Write to me. Tell me what's going on. Seems like nobody here writes about our neck of the woods unless there's big trouble brewing—and then they blow it up like they were talking about a catastrophe in a foreign country. They listen to me speak, and they look at me like I was from a foreign country. Worse even. You say you're from Birmingham—it's like having a scarlet letter on your chest.

How's the weather down there? The trees should be in bloom already. Up here the winter doesn't seem to want to let up. And not a magnolia in sight.

Dwayne

April 6, 1959

Dear Samuel,

Well, here I am in Cresson, Pa. Where in the world is that, you might ask? Check your map. Just north of Altoona, smack dab in the middle of the state. Unloaded some merchandise in Altoona and got here in time for a first day cover celebrating Robert Perry—fifty years of Arctic exploration. It's cold enough here. Why would anyone want to travel to the North Pole? You know, there was a black man in Perry's exploration group. Seems like blacks manage to get into just about everything. Equal craziness, if you ask me. I'm not sure why they're celebrating Arctic exploration in Cresson, Pa. Maybe one of the explorers was born here. Small-town USA. Good wholesome American values. But they do have a store that sells imported rugs—and a store that sells adult paraphernalia. I'm heading south after this—to Washington DC. There's a conference there that interests me. More on that later.

I met a woman in the adult store. A bit unusual. One woman among all those men. She seemed perfectly comfortable being there—buying a vibrator no less. That was intriguing. It turned out she was a local. She didn't seem to care who saw her there. You'd never see something like that back home. The ladies there would be more discrete. That takes some getting used to up here. Sex is open. Sentiment about blacks seems to be discrete. Back home ladies act with gentility, except if a black child tries to enroll in their children's school. Then the language that comes out of their mouths would make a sailor blush.

I chatted with this liberated woman—with the vibrator in plain sight on the counter. I invited her out to dinner at a Greek restaurant—the only one in town. A bit of exotic fare for what might prove to be an exotic encounter. Not much else to do in such a small town except maybe go to a bar and take the edge off loneliness and homesickness. Then again, what I miss about home seems to be disappearing fast. Maybe it was never quite there in the first place.

April 20, 1959

Dear Samuel,

Our nation's capital—although to listen to the folks back home it might as well be the bailiwick of an invading army. The War Between the States was supposed to have ended nearly a century ago. Ask my father about that. He'd be ready to secede tomorrow if it would mean keeping one dark face from sullying the lily-white walkways of the university. The schools. The lunch counters. He'd be the first to sign the Southern Manifesto if he could. Charter member of the White Citizens' Council—of the Orval Faubus fan club. The Feds have no business messing with the buses in Montgomery. We don't give a damn about the buses in New York City. Just leave us the hell alone, and we'll take care of our own business.

Notice the stamp. Seventeenth Congress of the International Chamber of Commerce. World Peace through World Trade. Nice slogan. The business leaders in our sister city seem to have realized that if you want to attract business from all over the country—from all over the world—you have to accommodate to changing times. It doesn't matter what you believe. It doesn't matter how you feel. The only color that matters is green. Build an airport big enough to accommodate planes flying in from Singapore and Nairobi, and when the folks get off the plane, act like you are glad they are here—whatever their color—as long as their wallets are full.

I have been going to the museums here. The Art Museum. The Smithsonian. Enough to keep me busy for weeks—if I didn't have business to attend to. Maybe I should have gotten here earlier instead of spending a week in Cresson, Pa. Cherchez la femme.

It was a good week in Cresson. My new friend showed me around, not that there was much to see. She told me the town history. The town secrets. You'd think that just because it is a small town in the middle of noplace that it wouldn't have secrets or scandals. People are pretty much the same wherever you go. I could write a novel just based on what she told me. Of course, I'd have to change the name of the town and the names of the people. Change their physical appearances somewhat. Still I imagine the people in a thousand small towns would protest that I was writing about them and that none of what I wrote was true anyway. The most interesting person of the lot was my friend. She is a clerk working for the city. Quiet, unassuming appearance. But under the cover of darkness—under the covers—a free spirit. Very free. Nothing like the proper ladies back home. No artifice. No restraint. A bit exhausting when all is said and done. The woman was attractive. No question about that. There was a small voice in my head that was telling me to look around and see if there were possibilities here. You don't meet someone like that every day. Then again, what could I offer her? She's not exactly the kind of woman you bring home to meet the folks. They would brand her. She would feel constrained—out of place. Even supposing I would want to bring anyone home to meet the folks—my father in particular. Even supposing I would still consider it home. Besides, she wasn't looking for anything permanent. She has a steady job with a good salary and good benefits. Occasionally she meets someone passing through who tickles her fancy. A bit of entertainment for a few days—a week at most. In between she takes care of her own needs. You've got to admire a person like that. Well, maybe yes, maybe no. I did. She made Cresson, Pa., more than a dot on the map. Trust one's fate. Go with the flow. Take one's adventures as they come. Be ready for anything.

MAY 1, 1959

Dear Samuel,

Denver. Why not? I've never been West of the Mississippi before. The drive was not terribly inspiring until I saw the mountains looming before me. We think the hills around town are imposing. That's what they are—hills. These are mountains. You walk the streets of this city, and you are higher than the highest hills of Alabama. And the mountains go up from there. Some are 14,000 feet above sea level. Those are real mountains.

The people—what can I say? They buy carpets and exotic toys the same as other folks. I got you the first day issue of the new stamp—a 4 1/2 cent coil stamp of Andrew Jackson and his residence, the Hermitage. What that has to do with Denver, I don't know. Jackson established his reputation in part as an Indian fighter. It depends on which side of the fence you're on whether you think that's good or bad. I don't think the Indians would think too highly of him—although they admired people who show courage in battle, even if they were the enemy. Funny the way different people responded to Western expansion. The Indians fought. They were massacred and put on reservations—on land so bad no one else wanted it. They kept their culture, and they were nearly wiped out. You listen to Indian music. It bears no resemblance at all to the music of the white man. You listen to the music of black people—it's not too far from the stuff white folks sang, hill folk. By and large, black people submitted to slavery. As bad as it was, most of them survived. Somewhere down the line, you get a reckoning for the choices you make. It's still not easy to be a black man, particularly in our neck of the woods. But some make it through and do pretty well for themselves. You see that here in Denver and up North. You don't get to see too many Indian people with homes in the suburbs—although maybe there are so many mixed breeds now, you can't tell. I don't know if that's a plus or not. Black people can't hide who they are—even those that are half and half, even a quarter. Either they make it being black, or they don't—although I'll tell you, some of them I've met are so light, you can't hardly tell. I can see why they'd want to pass. Even up North they don't have an easy time of it. And even if you pass, you can have a kid that's dark or has kinky hair.

I may stick around here a while. Sales are good. I can't get enough of the mountains. And I met this woman. Fresh as a daisy. A lot of women around here like that. They just open to the sunshine like flowers. No pretentions. They are just what they are, take it or leave it. Or in my case, take it and then leave it. I might feel a twinge of guilt afterward. I think they just assume that if you're interested, it must mean the whole package—marriage and family. At this point, I am a rambling man. I can't see myself opening a store and settling down. Carpets and the other stuff. If that's all I have to offer somebody, it can't be enough. Not in the long run. I don't think I've been around long enough for her to care that much about my moving on. I never promised her a rose garden.

May 15, 1959

Dear Samuel,

I'm back in New York. I'm putting a lot of mileage on my vehicle. I hope it holds up. I can't really afford to buy a new one.

I renewed my stock. Some interesting carpets from Belgium. Not quite up to the Romanian stuff, but then again the prices are better. Most people are not sticklers for authenticity. If it's close enough, they'll bite. The appearance of good taste to show off to their neighbors. At times they wind up paying as much for appearance as for the real thing.

The UN is celebrating the Economic Commission for Europe. I'm not sure what this is all about. I read somewhere that they were trying to monitor coal and steel production to make sure one nation or another wouldn't try surreptitiously to arm for war like the Germans did back in the '30s. It might be that. Or maybe Europe might be gearing up to take on the U.S. economically. I'm not really up on economic theory. You listen to these economists talking about a problem, and it's as if they're all talking a different language.

I went back to the market area on the Lower East Side. Great energy there. Hustle and bustle. I actually feel myself walking faster when I'm there. You don't walk fast, and people look like they're ready to run over you—and that's on the sidewalk. The streets are something else. The cabs race around like they were driving in La Mans or Indy. Sometimes it seems like they're aiming at you when you cross the street. But I've managed to survive so far. A few close calls. Nothing to get excited about.

Meanwhile my van is loaded to the gills. I'll be headed out early. There is a lot of breaking into cars in the city, and I can't afford to lose any stock. I'm not insured for anything—especially not the Danish stuff.

May 30, 1959

Dear Samuel,

DC. They're celebrating the Lincoln Sesquicentennial with a four-cent stamp. I'm sure people remember that all over Dixie. They'd probably rather celebrate the date of his assassination—maybe the birthday of John Wilkes Booth.

I spent some time at the Lincoln Memorial. Impressive. No comment for Jefferson Davis. The winners get all the honors. They get to write the history books. Then again I remember the book I had to read in school about the War of Northern Aggression. It's only been a hundred years. Give people a little longer to get over it. The South will rise again. The South is rising—not the way some people would like. Atlanta is rising again. Give it another century, and maybe we will too.

I was standing next to a woman at the monument. She was looking up at the statue as if Lincoln were some kind of God—a saint at the very least. The look of veneration in her eyes. Well, I suppose everyone has to have someone to adulate. I still haven't found anyone. Is that why I'm wandering so aimlessly? I read somewhere that you can meet your next teacher anywhere. Your next guru. So I guess I'm going anywhere to meet him—or her. It could just as easily be a woman. I might actually prefer it, especially if she had good looks to go along with her wisdom and insight. Someone who could hold my interest for more than a few weeks at a time.

June 3, 1959

Dear Samuel,

Oxford, Ohio. They're honoring Benjamin Harrison of all people. OK, he was the 23rd President. But who remembers anything he did? It's the 150th anniversary of his birth. I'll bet if you asked people to name the 23rd President, not one in a hundred could come up with the right answer, let alone remember the year he was born. There was a time when I knew all the Presidents in order. I surely don't remember them now. The envelope says he went to college in Miami of Ohio. Another tidbit of useless information.

Now if they wanted to really get interesting, they could issue some commemorative stamps about events and people that were more striking. How about a stamp commemorating the first anniversary of the bombing of Shuttlesworth's church in Birmingham? Or the fifth anniversary of Brown vs. the Board of Education, which rejected the concept of separate but "equal." Or the second anniversary of the boycotting of Nat King Cole's concert of "jungle music" or the Prayer Pilgrimage for Freedom in DC or the ninth anniversary of the McLaurin vs. Oklahoma State Regents? Or the Sweatt vs. Painter and Henderson vs. the United States ruling on railroad dining cars, law schools, and colleges. I bet my father would buy up all the stamps he could get a hold of—and burn them—maybe in Ingram Park, dressed all in white like his buddies. Oxford, Ohio, doesn't offer much besides the university. I have another major trip ahead of me. Another swing out West. More later.

June 8, 1959

Dear Samuel,

I'm in Virginia City, Nevada. The hundredth anniversary of the Comstock Lode. Boomtown. Maybe like Birmingham in the 1870s and 1880s. Not gold or silver. Coal, limestone, and iron ore. Birmingham. Steel Town. The Pittsburgh of the South. Except that now the furnaces are being shut down. Cheaper foreign steel. Will Birmingham become a ghost town? Maybe build up a great Medical Center. That's the ticket. We'll get all those doctors and scientists to come to town—white ward to the left, black to the right. White blood in this facility, black blood in that. What to do with mixed blood? No such thing. One drop of black blood is all it takes. One drop. The way I hear tell, that would include just about everyone. If they had a test, some people would be unpleasantly surprised. Third cousin once removed. Removed from schools. From lunch counters. Swimming pools. Around here, that didn't seem to be a problem. You have the money, you can buy booze anywhere. Booze and women. The only color they care about is green. I think I wrote that to you before. Money is the great equalizer. You got it, you white. You don't, you're a nigger. Simple as that.

June 17, 1959

Dear Samuel,

I'm back East again. A more leisurely trip than the trip out. Got a chance to see more of the country, not that Kansas is all that exciting. Kansas, Iowa, Nebraska, Tennessee, Kentucky—not all that bad. West Virginia. Up through Pennsylvania. Nice mountains. Winding roads. Up through New York State and finally to Boston. In time for the celebration of the anniversary of the Battle of Bunker Hill. Read up on that. We came within a whisper of losing the War. That would have been interesting. Under the British thumb for another hundred years. The British had a southern strategy. Offer the slaves their freedom if they'd fight against the rebels. The Americans had a northern strategy—offer slaves their freedom if they fought on the side of the Colonists. Not that all colonists were in favor of independence. At first it was just an organized minority. That's the way most things get started—with a vocal minority. You take a poll at the time, and the majority either favors the status quo or doesn't want to get involved. So don't tell me about polls on any current issues. It doesn't really matter which way the majority votes. They aren't going to determine anything. It doesn't matter whether you're talking about American independence or integrating schools. The same people that would foam at the mouth yesterday will shrug their shoulders tomorrow and forget what the furor was about.

Funny though—the British didn't change. They said the same thing about people trying to win independence in India as they did about the American colonists years earlier. And they had to bow out more or less gracefully years before they thought the natives were ready for self-rule. I'm not sure the Indians are doing that much better under self-rule. Only now they've got no one else to blame but themselves.

Four days in the Boston area before I head back to NYC. Boston has a reputation for being cultural—and somewhat prudish. The culture part is obvious. I went to a concert of Baroque music played on period instruments. I probably would have enjoyed it more if they had played modern instruments, but they wanted to be . . . authentic, whatever that means these days. The prudish part supposedly has to do with reaction to porn (all the juicy stuff is banned in Boston). I didn't find that to be true. The adult bookstores were always crowded. I did very well in Boston, as far as sales were concerned.

And . . . I picked up someone at a bar. Brought her back to my room for some extended conversation—which of course led to more than mere conversation. Much more. She was a free spirit. Enjoy the moment, and once it's over, just let it go. Actually a few moments. A few days. A few nights. I wouldn't have minded staying a bit longer, but she seemed happy enough with my initial time schedule. No desire on her part for a long-term relationship. I understood that. I really did. But I wouldn't have minded more. A week or two. Maybe a month. With someone that educated. If I can't say that I got an education at Harvard, it would be rewarding to spend time with someone who did. Rub up against culture, especially if it comes in such a pretty package. Thank God for Bunker Hill. Hip, hip, hooray for the American War of Independence.

June 23, 1959

Dear Samuel,

Back in NYC. For some reason they're celebrating something called Dixipix II in Birmingham. They're supposed to be issuing a four-cent stamp of the U.S. flag. Liberty. The pride of Birmingham. I won't be coming to Birmingham for the occasion. Certainly not to celebrate whatever it is that they're calling liberty—or whatever else they're proud of. You can write to me about the exhibition at your leisure—go to the Post Office and get the first day of issue. The American flag. Not the flag of the Confederacy. Tell the Reverend Shuttlesworth about Liberty and the pride of Birmingham. Tell the members of his church. Maybe they'll want to celebrate the first anniversary of Eisenhower's statement about enforcing federal laws in the Deep South. Poor Eisenhower. He had an easier time of it planning and carrying out the invasion of Normandy than dealing with Arkansas and Alabama. Dixipix II. Interesting. I missed Dixipix I. Is it an annual affair? Open to the public? All the public? Do they have separate days for white and black?

I heard an interesting story up here from two Southern boys of the dark persuasion. They were tired of Jim Crow. They tried an experiment. They got dressed up in foreign-looking robes and put on some kind of fake accent. They had no trouble breaking through the color line in all kinds of places. It seems that the locals were only interested in separating the races in people who were American born. Foreigners didn't count. What would happen if suddenly all blacks got dressed up and sounded like foreigners? What would Daddy's buddies do then? How long would it take them to realize they'd been had? It took a lot of guts for those two to pull the caper off—to pretend they didn't know their way around. They actually asked a cop for directions. They sat in the front of the bus without any problem—talking a bunch of gibberish they passed off as a foreign language. No one asked them to move. They were no different to the other riders than if they had been Frenchmen.

I wonder what would have happened if they were dressed normally and spoke French and seemed not to understand what was being said when they were told to move to the back of the bus. That would have been chancier. There are blacks in France. French citizens, no less. I don't know if any of them have traveled to Birmingham. Maybe the Mayor could give them special dispensation. They could wear a badge around their necks—honored citizen of France. Don't hassle us, or you will cause an international incident. Or maybe citizens of France—to be treated like any other Frenchman. Not that the folks back home particularly like Frenchmen of any color. Maybe they could have a police escort to explain to the local yokels—these men aren't really black, even though they look black. They're really French. Just listen to them talk. Don't confuse them with the local niggers. In any case, they're only visiting for a few days, and we can trust the fact they won't be making eyes at any of our Southern belles. Heaven forbid—even if they mess with lily-white French girls back home. You know the French. No respect for separation of the races. Can't even interpret the Bible properly. Don't mix two different seeds in the same field. How clear can you get? Then again, what can you expect from a couple of Catholics?

I'll be staying around here for a few days and then head upstate near the Canadian border. They're celebrating the opening of the St. Lawrence Seaway in Massena, New York.

June 29, 1959

Dear Samuel,

New York State is quite beautiful. In many ways it reminds me of the landscape in northern Alabama. Rolling hills. Not quite the same. I still experience pangs of nostalgia, especially when I hear people speak. The music of the words is different. Even the vocabulary. The pace that they walk. The way they address you. I would give anything to hear someone say, "Bless your Heart," at least once when they talk to me. I remember the words of the prophet—"How can I sing in a strange land. I sat by the waters of Babylon and I wept. If I forget thee, o Jerusalem, may my right hand lose its cunning—may my tongue cleave to the roof of my mouth." But Birmingham isn't quite Jerusalem, is it? At least in theory. I could return anytime I want to. I don't have to wait seventy years. My exile is a chosen one. Is there someone at home who, like Rachael, will weep at my absence?

The Hebrew people in exile used to wrap themselves in prayer shawls with a thread of blue at each corner. The thread of blue was colored with a dye made from a shellfish from the Mediterranean Sea that was not found in Babylonia. There were other blue dyes available in Babylonia. The people chose not to use them. And when the cost of importing blue threads from the homeland became prohibitively expensive, or the process of obtaining the dye was lost, the absence of the blue thread reminded them every day that they were in exile. By the time a remnant returned to the Holy Land, the process had in fact been lost, so that even in their own land, they were reminded every day that something was missing. You can't go home again—or at least when you return, you realize it is not quite the same. Perhaps the reason most of the people chose to stay in a foreign land was that it was better to remain in exile than to be reminded of what was lost back home.

And so, here I am, in Massena, New York. Celebrating or at least noting what for them was a significant technological event—the opening of a waterway that would vastly improve the economic development of the area for all people. Would that I could celebrate something like that back home that would vastly improve the economic development of all the people of Birmingham. The mines are closing. The steel mills are shutting down. The medical center of national and international renown will certainly benefit all those fine folks who will live over the mountains in polite little suburbs, where, after the evening sun goes down, they will not have to see the squalor that lies at the heart of the city—on the other side of the tracks. The poverty. The anguish. The desperation.

So, here I am, a thousand miles away. I sat by the waters of the St. Lawrence Seaway. And I wept.

July 4, 1959

Dear Samuel,

I'm still in New York State. Auburn. Yes. There is an Auburn here too. Check your map. Just west of Syracuse. For some reason they are celebrating the 49th state to earn a star on the flag here. Somehow Alabama is still included as an integral part of the U.S. Maybe one day it will act accordingly.

Sales are going well. People readily buy reproductions of the real thing to reflect their good taste at bargain prices. The other merchandise are also selling well. Spice up one's life without shocking one's sensibilities too much. Let people enjoy their lives a bit more without thinking they are flagrantly immoral. I may have saved a few marriages that were sinking into monotony. Preventing a few spouses from thinking adultery was the only option they had to deal with the humdrum existence they were leading.

The climate is rather pleasant. I have a personal guide to show me the beauties of the countryside. A guide who is beautiful in her own right and is not adverse to going on some exotic adventures of her own along the way. What can I say? I enjoy the company of women. Exotic women, if you will. Women. Not ladies. Although probably even some of our Southern belles can allow themselves to act like women once the shades are drawn, I do declare.

A pleasant interlude for a rambling man. That may be one of the things women find intriguing in me. They can let their hair down, as it were, and not have to factor in everything they do as part of a lasting relationship. Let their inhibitions go, and no one else will be the wiser for it—once I hit the road.

And me—will I ever get to the point where I'm ready for more than pleasant interludes, brief excursions into new landscapes, an eternal tourist. Will I ever be able to settle down and call some place home? A place like Auburn, NY. Not yet. I'll spend a few weeks here—why not? And then I'll be heading west—to Lafayette, Indiana. I'll write to you once I get there.

AUGUST 17, 1959

Dear Samuel

I hear the Klan has been kicking up its heels. Cross burnings. Parades. Bombings. You wouldn't think it, but the Klan was big around here thirty some odd years ago. Really. The big issue here then was religion, not race. Al Smith was running for President. He was Catholic. The Klan back then hated Catholics as much as it hated blacks and Jews. Not that there aren't strong feelings about blacks here. I've been riding around the state. Southern Indiana is like the Deep South on matters of race. I actually saw a sign on a state highway outside one town that read, "the sun never sat on a nigger in this town." Can you imagine? The only one lower than a black around these parts is a migrant worker from Kentucky. The stories they tell about Kentucky folk would make your hair curl. Someone told me a joke the other day. "What do you call a Kentucky man that marries a black woman?" Answer—a social climber. Up north near Chicago, the racial climate is also pretty rough. It seems that back in the '20s, industrialists tried to break the back of the union movement by hiring scab labor—mostly up from the South. People don't seem to remember those workers were both white and black. I guess the blacks were more visible. Back home you get cities where blacks live on the other side of the railroad tracks—where the pavements and streetlights end. It's not that different in cities like Gary. It may be rougher than Birmingham. None of the civility that at least acts like a façade. Not that the Klan is much on civility. I guess if you scratch most people right, the civility disappears, and you get a mob shouting for someone's blood—especially if the people in the mob can cover their faces with a mask so nobody can figure out who you are. Then after you burn a cross or two, scare the piss out of a few people, maybe lynch one or two for being too uppity, you can go back home, go to church, weed the garden, coach a Little League baseball team—whatever. Around here the big thing is basketball. They have a high school championship—people get more excited about that than the World Series. And college basketball. Ten times more the thrill.

And hot air balloons. They started the first airmail service here by hot air balloon. A piece of information most people don't remember.

They have a big university here. Purdue. It specializes in fields like Engineering. The campus is integrated to some degree. No one seems to give it much mind. Maybe someday back home. Maybe. I should live so long.

September 29, 1959

Dear Samuel,

I'm back in DC. I do well in Washington—and the suburbs. No one seems to live in Washington proper. They've got money to burn—no semblance of inhibition. So I'm doing well. Really well. If I stay around here for any length of time, I could live high off the hog.

The stamp on the First Day Cover honors the Mayor of Berlin, Germany, as a Champion of Liberty. I'll admit to you that I never heard of him before. I guess it must have something to do with the Cold War and Communism. The Berlin Wall kept people from East Germany from escaping to the West, where people had more freedom and a better economy. The picture on the stamp makes the Mayor look black, but that is hardly likely. The Germans had their own ideas on race. Aryans on top, blacks way down the list—Jews, gypsies, homosexuals, and mental defectives just vermin to be eliminated. We never quite got to that level. I'm sure there are people who wouldn't mind stringing up all the homosexuals they could find—and anybody who bucks the system that they could label as a Communist. You wouldn't want Communists in your neighborhood, would you?

So, how long would it take for the U.S. Postal Service to honor the Mayor of Birmingham as a Champion of Liberty? Take down the wall! I heard that they were supposed to integrate eighteen schools in Jefferson County. How did that go?

Jefferson County. Named for Thomas Jefferson. One of the framers of the Constitution. He owned slaves. Was even supposed to have had children with one of his slaves. It figures. OK, he was supposed to have said the country would eventually have to deal with the problem of slavery—later. Not in his time. Typical. As great as he was, he couldn't figure out how to work out that problem. It would take someone at least as great as he was to work things out now—nearly two centuries later. Ah well.

October 23, 1959

Dear Samuel,

I'm back in NYC. Time to get resupplied. There's an American company that makes fake Oriental carpets made with synthetic fibers. They're selling out of fancy department stores. I suppose there is a good market for that, but my carpets are 100% wool and are handwoven—at about the same price. I sell to stores that won't touch synthetic fabrics that are machine-woven, no matter how good they look and how well they wear. There's enough room for them and me. And the other stuff I carry. No complaints there either. The same folks that complain about how the country is sinking into sin seem to get off on a bit of fancy nookie on the side.

I had to work a bit trying to understand the stamp from the UN that I'm sending you. UN Day. OK, that was easy. But the Plebiscite in British Togoland under UN Trusteeship was a bit trickier. So I looked it up.

Togo is this tiny country in West Africa. Until 1918 it was a German colony. Germany lost all of its foreign colonies after it was defeated in World War I. That's when things begin to get a bit crazy. The Allies wanted the colonies that Germany lost—places like Southwest Africa and Tanzanika. OK, you could understand trying to reclaim large areas of land. But Togoland is this little strip of land—not worth fighting about. There was this strange figure named Marcus Garvey. Up from Jamaica. He was into radical stuff. He thought there was no hope for black people in America. He wanted to take them all back to Africa—wanted to start black businesses and gain power through money. Not such a wild idea. He organized a couple million followers. Not the cultural elite—ordinary people. Marched down Fifth Avenue in a parade where he rode on a horse dressed in some outlandish military costume. Got a whole bunch of people really scared.

He had this idea that black people in Africa could run their own affairs, could lead independent nations—throw off the yoke of colonialism and show the world that Africans were equal to anyone.

He thought Togoland was as good a place as any to start with. It was small—pretty insignificant by all standards, not worth batting an eyelash over. It was plagued with malaria and sleeping sickness. So why not try a grand experiment—turn Togoland over to the Africans to run it. Show the world. Start a movement for independence that might lead to independence of the colonies. He wrote somewhere that once blacks had power, the same people that called African men "boy" today would call them "sir" tomorrow—to get at the natural resources. You can imagine that didn't go over big with the Europeans. The Americans managed to get Garvey deported. The Europeans split the country in half—gave one part to the British and one part to the French—and now we have a stamp from the UN to celebrate this wonderful decision. Ironic, wasn't it? I wonder what would have happened back then if they had made Togoland an independent country. You read the literature about Africa back then, look at the old movies—*Tarzan of the Apes*, *Ramar of the Jungle*. All you see is Africans running around half-naked talking mumbo-jumbo and shaking spears at each other. Hardly the kind of folks you'd want to see running a country of any size. I guess that's the same image you got about blacks in this country during Reconstruction. A bunch of near illiterates protected by carpetbaggers and bleeding hearts, lording it over the poor Confederate whites after they lost the Civil War—or rather the War of Northern Aggression. Call it what you will—Lincoln's Republican Party rubbing the nose of the losers into the horse manure of defeat. It doesn't take long for the South to rise again and put the niggers in their place. Funny thing now. Up here just about all the blacks vote Democratic—after FDR. You'd think he was a prophet to God, leading them all to the Promised Land. Back home it's another story.

I hear tell that blacks are getting organized now. The Alabama Christian Movement for Civil Rights. And they are demanding—demanding no less that all public parks and recreation centers be integrated. And the Federal Courts are going along with all this. Whites are getting organized as well. The Klan is marching through black neighborhoods. It isn't finding any difficulties getting parade permits. They're burning their crosses here and there. No fear of getting arrested for what they do. And Bull is threatening to close all the parks and recreation centers rather than have little white children play with little black children. We couldn't have things like that happen. I mean, you get kids playing with each other, and they might actually like each other—accept each other as being just . . . kids. That would never do. The next thing you'd have is blacks and whites sitting next to each other in church discovering that they were both Christians of the same persuasion. And the whole edifice of society would start to crumble. You wouldn't want your sister to marry one of those people, would you? Go against the Bible, the very word of God, who warned about sowing different seeds in the same field—the curse of Ham and all that. Like the sermon I once heard as a child—even the Devil can quote Scripture. I never understood what that meant back then. I guess you can prove just about anything if you select your passages carefully. I came across one passage where it said that if you found a runaway slave, you were not to return him to his master. That you were to provide him with the means for him to set up his own household. Really. It says that in Scripture. All those Bible-quoting folks missed that passage when they passed the Fugitive Slave Law and got it supported by the Supreme Court. Other passages say that if you injure the eye or the tooth of your slave, the slave goes free and you have to pay him damages for the injury he sustained.

Amazing what you can find in Scripture. I suppose the fact that you find slavery in the Bible justifies the perpetuation of that peculiar institution. But there's all kinds of stuff in there about protecting female slaves from sexual abuse—even while they could be used as breeding stock for the Master, as property to be handed down from father to son. I'm no Biblical scholar. I get confused by all these contradictions. I'm not much of a churchgoer these days. I stopped going when the Minister of our church back home started preaching about God and segregation. Maybe I should give it a try up here. But I'm moving around so much, there's no church I could call home. Maybe once I settle down—if I ever do. I'll be in New York for a while, but I don't think I could ever call this place home. Too big. Too noisy. Although I'm telling you—this place has museums and libraries and such that could make your head spin. The public library is so big, you could get lost in it. I had to spend a whole day figuring out how to get the information I wanted on Togoland. Some interesting types here sitting next to each other without a thought of whether it was weird rubbing elbows with such folk. But everything in New York is all packed together. And everybody rushes around so fast, there's no time to pay attention to who's coming by then. Not like back home, where the railroad tracks divide everything pretty much into us and them.

November 20, 1959

Dear Samuel,

It's winter here. OK—not according to the calendar. But the weather is already nasty. That takes some getting used to. I've been here over a month, and I'm getting ready to move again. Maybe a little south, where the weather is a bit milder. Notice the stamp. U.S. Airmail. Liberty for All. Well, maybe up here, if you define Liberty carefully enough. The freedom of some folks to make sure other folks don't define their freedom their way. Part of American history. Way back when. Did you know that back in Colonial times, you could get thrown in jail in Massachusetts if you professed the "wrong" religion or the "wrong" set of beliefs. It was like that in most of the Colonies. If you were Catholic, almost the only place you could live safely was in Maryland—at least for a while. We like to talk about the Four Freedoms. One is Freedom of Religion. It wasn't true back then—until the Constitution—and even the Constitution didn't eliminate slavery. Didn't give women the right to vote. I guess it was a beginning. The start of a long process. So maybe the stamp is less a commemoration of what was and is than a hope for what will be—hopefully. Anyway, it's a stamp. First day of issue. You can add it to your collection.

I'm writing this letter to you from a park bench. It's so cold, I can hardly hold the pen. I'm going somewhere where I can get some hot coffee. I don't think I'll ever get used to the weather here. I guess there's a price to be paid for everything you do.

December 3, 1959

Dear Samuel,

I'm here in Danville, Kentucky—about 25 miles south of Lexington. The stamp celebrates the first successful abdominal surgery recorded anywhere—back in 1809. Dr. Ephraim McDowell. I wonder who researched that. Back in 1809 they didn't know about germs, so they would do their surgeries and people would die a few days later from infection. You'd think they could have come up with something in a major hospital in a big city. Then again, I read about hospitals and childbirth. It said big city hospitals were more dangerous for women than little hospitals in small towns. The docs in the teaching hospitals would go from autopsies of women who had died to doing exams on living patients without washing their hands or wearing gloves. That just boggles my mind. What passed for standard medical practice only a few years ago—and the doctors themselves resisted any effort to make them wash their hands. Birmingham is trying to build medical facilities to rival the best facilities anywhere in the world. I guess if you could make a name for yourself in Danville, Kentucky, you could do it in Birmingham. I'm not sure the city is ready to welcome all the docs that would come with open arms—at least the docs that were swarthy. Docs tend to live in nice neighborhoods and send their kids to the best schools. So they can become docs when they grow up. So maybe the swarthy ones will choose to go somewhere else. Wouldn't want to rock the boat too much. Not with Bull keeping the lid on things. Kentucky is nice—a bit more Southern than what I've been getting used to of late. A bit more . . . familiar—friendly. I could get used to a small town, where everybody knows your name. Close enough to a big city for entertainment and business. Got some sales in Lexington. Not much in Danville. Simple folk. Not much sophistication when it comes to putting a rug down. If it covers the floor and the color matches the curtains, it's just fine and dandy. Not too many people willing to pay more for something exotic or refined. Not too many people willing to get exotic in the bedroom either. If missionary position was good enough for grandpa, it's good enough for me. And all this other stuff I'm peddling. If it's not explicitly forbidden in the Bible, it feels like it ought to be. Lexington is better in that regard. Louisville still better than that. I don't need too many sophisticated folks around to make a living. And here in Kentucky, at least in the bigger cities, there's enough folks around to make it worth my while. And some of the sophisticated ones are really beautiful women who like nice carpets and don't mind hearing about the paraphernalia I handle. There are some real pleasures involved in the business. I got to demonstrate some of the wares I sell—as long as I am discreet about it. And I am discreet I give away some free samples along the way. Not bad for business. I let my clients spread the word. Satisfied customers in more ways than one.

December 10, 1959

Dear Samuel,

I am back in New York. The stamp from the UN commemorates World Refugee Year. I wasn't aware that we were commemorating refugees. I will admit to you that I couldn't enumerate which refugees we were commemorating. That's the problem. The world is so vast. The problems are so numerous that one can only begin to notice those that are close to home. I admire people who can pinpoint areas of need somewhere in the world and can drop everything else and go there to help better the situation. I can't even begin to see how the situation in my hometown can be fixed. So I float around selling carpets and sex toys hither and yon. OK, people get happy if their homes look pretty. Maybe I save a few marriages here and there. Maybe I break up a few marriages as well. Who knows? But this hardly constitutes a purpose for living. I guess I hoped that traveling around would give me some kind of insight—a sense of direction in my life. That hasn't happened yet. The year is drawing to a close. The decade is drawing to a close. Time for resolution. I don't know where to begin. I don't even have a clue.

I hear that a Federal judge is going to be giving a ruling soon on the question of integrating interstate buses—maybe city buses as well. I think he's the same one that ruled on other integration cases before, so there's little doubt as to what he will rule this time, not that it makes any difference. The Feds can rule any way they want. As long as enforcement is in the hands of state and local officials, it will be like spitting in the wind. I wanted to say pissing in the wind. It comes to the same thing.

JANUARY 20, 1960

Dear Samuel,

Mt. Vernon, Virginia. As good as any place to honor the Father of the Country. A series of stamps to be issued defining the American Credo. I didn't know we had a Credo as such. I don't know who gets to choose which words of wisdom they culled from everything Washington said or wrote. The quote says, "Observe good faith and justice to all nations." It says nothing about good faith and justice to the inhabitants of one's own nation. We put a good face on for the rest of the world. We are a democracy. We hold to certain ideals—the four freedoms, et al. But when it comes to our own citizens, that's another question—even defining them as citizens. Blacks are only 3/5 of a person according to the Constitution. Native Americans are less. Injuns. The only good Injun is a dead Injun. They can't vote. They can't influence governmental policy to their own people. Most black folk can't vote either—at least in our neck of the woods. It's all done legal-like. Poll taxes. Literacy tests. If you're white, you get to spell "CAT" and name the state you live in. If you're black, you have to spell "CHRYSANTHEMUM" and repeat the third sentence of the fifteenth paragraph of the state constitution—verbatim. And en route going or coming, you get to see one of your neighbors promise to burn a cross in your front yard, because you're being so uppity. Obvious good will. Good faith. Justice. And when the Feds step in, locals talk about States' Rights and what happened during Reconstruction. They get their hackles raised with righteous indignation about how the Yankees are trying to destroy our noble institutions—our way of life—and would you want your sister to marry a Nigrah?

I walked around Mt. Vernon. Impressive. The founding fathers were an impressive group—of white men. Into philosophy, architecture, sciences, art, and music. And they lived well. Big plantation homes—with slaves, of course. Talk about good faith and justice for all. I walk through a home like this. Everyone oohs and aahs. After all, this is where George Washington lived—the Father of our Country. The man who turned down the suggestion that he become a king.

Who would not serve more than two terms as President because he thought that would be undemocratic. Big monument to the man in DC. Part of me wanted to be impressed. Part of me wanted to puke. All those fine words. If he had believed them, really, deep down inside. If he had had the balls to stand up to those slavers way back when—he and the other Founding Fathers—this would be a different country now. Why don't people see that? Maybe, symbolically spit on the floor of this well-kept mansion. Maybe piss in a corner. An act of sacrilege perhaps. One man's sacrilege is another man's protest. So they arrest me. Fine me. Jail me for a weekend. Didn't Thoreau say that the only place for an honest man in the face of injustice was in prison? And he went to prison—at least overnight. He wouldn't pay taxes to a government that maintained the slave system and was fighting what he considered to be an unjust war. One of his friends bailed him out, paid his back taxes—about $1.24 if I remember correctly—so Thoreau could go back to his pond and contemplate the world of nature again. Better to watch hawks pounce on field mice than to watch people oppress each other.

I visited a plantation in Louisiana a few years back. Another impressive house filled with fine furnishings, mostly shipped over from Europe. The owners lived high off the hog while the sugar cane cutters were earning less than $2 a day. You are supposed to go to the manor house and admire all the fancy stuff. I asked for a tour of the workers' shacks. That wasn't part of the tour. I stayed outside and waited for the others to finish. I couldn't trust myself to be a nice little visitor and not destroy at least one small thing—symbolically of course. Funny thing. Not all the workers were black. It turns out the swamps were cleared by German immigrants. They came much cheaper than slaves. So much for all this hogwash about racism. If the price was right, a planter was just as happy oppressing a white man. Put him in malarial swamps to get things ready for the Massah and his family to move into the Big House and live like royalty. The immigrants died like flies. Someone told me 90% in the first year. They got promised 40 acres and a mule if they survived seven years. You knew most of them wouldn't. White Christians putting a number on other White Christians. Treating them worse than blacks, because slaves were expensive by then. All a question of money, not race. We'd solve the whole problem right off if we could convince the powers that be that it was profitable to be human. That's what they're doing in Atlanta. They're going to leave us in the dust. Forget all this crap about black men lusting after white women. It's all a question of money. Besides, there were certainly enough white men getting their rocks off at the expense of black women. Generation after generation. Some of the children are lighter skinned than their fathers. There will come a time when none of this color crap will matter one tinker's damn. Money will marry money or the prospects of money, and no one will give it a second thought. That's my American Credo. I don't think they'll ever put that on a Commemorative Stamp. Not in my lifetime.

February 8, 1960

Dear Samuel,

Washington DC again. New stamps. Fiftieth Anniversary of the Boy Scouts of America. That's OK. A good thing for boys to get into outdoor stuff—hiking and camping. Tying knots. Figuring out what to eat as you wander through the woods. Big news out of North Carolina. Four black students sit in at a lunch counter in Greensboro. Ask to be served. They are refused of course. Then arrested. More students showed up to take their place. What is it going to come to? Arrest the entire black community before it's over. Build some new prisons to accommodate them? I think we're in for some rough times ahead. This is the beginning of something new. The blacks won't kowtow to the whites anymore—bow and scrape and say, "Yessuh," "Yes, massah," "Yes, yes, Miss Anne." I know what the powers that be will say. Our blacks are happy and content. It is just a few outside agitators stirring things up. We can handle those few easily enough. Then things will quiet down like they were before. Just take care of those agitators. Take care of them good. Especially the white ones. Traitors to their race. What's the world coming to? What indeed!

February 18, 1960

Dear Samuel,

You said to chill out a bit. I am chilling out in Olympic Village, California. It took 4 1/2 days of hard driving to get out here for the Winter Olympics. You know how much I like sporting events—any sporting events. I once watched a championship tiddly-winks contest. Really. Hours and hours to determine the winner. If I could watch that, then certainly ski jumping would hold my interest. Figure skating. Any number of events. The world is invited to participate. Strangely I haven't seen any black athletes. It's as if the games were being held in Birmingham and the Bull were running the show. I realize that can't be true. This is California. They don't do things like that here. OK, there are Asians here. But Bull doesn't give a damn about Asians. Hardly a black face among the spectators. It's a bit uncanny. I guess if you can't find your own among the competitors, it's not worth the trouble to come out. Funny thing how different groups go out for different sports. But if you can box or hit a baseball, you should be able to ski down a hill. No Jackie Robinsons here.

News from North Carolina now followed up in Tennessee. Nashville. Sit-ins. It won't be long before it comes to Alabama. Then the fireworks will begin. I can't understand what the fuss is about. You want to eat a hamburger. Who the Hell cares who is sitting next to you. A hamburger is a hamburger. No big deal. You can still invite whoever you want to your house for dinner.

The news came out yesterday that an Alabama Grand Jury indicted Martin Luther King Jr. for tax evasion. If they think that will stop the sit-ins and demonstrations, that's downright stupid. I know the routine. You stop some black man for driving with a busted tail light. Next thing you know you find some drugs or illegal gun you planted in his trunk. You throw him in jail. His car mysteriously disappears. That stuff worked thirty years ago. Not anymore. I'm sure King has enough hot-shot lawyers to run circles around the Yahoos that are trying to stop him. Hot-shot New York lawyers that will make our good ol' boys look like the bumpkins they really are.

You don't stop a rampaging elephant by jabbing at him with toothpicks. That just gets his dander up. And there's a lot of dander to get up. Like trying to stop a runaway train with a two-by-four. I shouldn't let myself get so riled up. Concentrate on the games. Not much on sales here. At least the carpets. The toys are something else. A lot of young people here. Adventurous young people looking for a good time. Into whatever the new fad might be. I convince them that the new fad on the East Coast is whatever I have to sell. It's a bit pricey, but hey, so is the price of a hotel room—and the food. For the price of a meal, you can satisfy some other needs, some of which you didn't even know you had. I like the young folks here. Little or no inhibitions. Always seeking new thrills. Not wanting to miss a thing. So I'm holding my own here. More than that.

A lot of the women don't want to make the effort to read the instructions. They want demonstrations. I'm performing a needed service. Promoting the general welfare. A new age. The women are seeking pleasure just like the men—not needing or even looking for the promise of love and commitment. There are more contests here than just on the playing field. I heard one guy bragging about six conquests in a single night. Conquest is the wrong word. It's not a conquest when your perspective partner is ready and willing. No contest at all. Before I leave, I expect to hear some sweet young thing brag that she made six conquests in one night. Maybe more. Women have certain advantages in the game of love. OK, the game of sex. There's no time for love. Sometimes no time even to find out a person's name.

February 29, 1960

Dear Samuel,

I'm back in New York. The UN celebrates the twelfth anniversary of its meeting in Chaillot, France. Twelve. Why not? Keep the commemoratives coming. The 5000th day anniversary.

Sit-ins in Richmond. I knew it would happen sooner or later. They picketed the Woolworth's in NYC—in sympathy. It's a national company. They should take a stand. If more companies had the balls to stand up to local Yahoos, all this nonsense would disappear in a matter of weeks. Let all the national chain stores threaten to boycott local towns. Lay off workers until the locals complied. Let the common folk feel the economic pinch. It won't happen. Businessmen won't buck the system for some ideal. The only ideal they hold to is today's bottom line. People only do what they think they have to do. No one does anything out of the goodness of their hearts.

March 6, 1960

Dear Samuel,

I am in Richmond. Things seem peaceful enough. They're holding the Third Annual Spring Meeting of the American Philatelic Society sponsored by the Richmond Stamp Club as if there were nothing more important to discuss than colored bits of paper used by the Feds to cover the cost of mailing a letter. They get excited about that. I asked some visitors from out of town, "Hey, did you hear about the sit-ins at Woolworth's two weeks ago?" They shrug their shoulders. If the world were coming to an end tomorrow, it wouldn't faze them one iota. Did you hear about the stamp I found in a garage sale in Madison, Wisconsin? A comet is headed directly toward Richmond. It will destroy all life forms except for roaches, ants, and bacteria for 300 miles around. Oh, really. Take a peek at this stamp. Isn't it a beauty? Only a thousand printed like this. And I have five copies. Just think. Five.

MARCH 7, 1960

Dear Samuel,

DC again. The suburbs have proved to be an open market for me. In the down time I visit the Smithsonian and the National Art Gallery. I could be here a few months and not see everything I want to. And this stamp comes out celebrating yet another Champion of Liberty. Thomas G. Masaryk, the first President of Czechoslovakia. Nice international perspective to honor those who fought for freedom—somewhere far enough away that we don't have to think much about the good ol' U.S. of A. So that we don't have to think about the student expelled from Vanderbilt University for participating in a demonstration. Talk about First Amendment freedoms. We don't have to think about the black guy in Houston who was beaten up, hanged upside down in a tree with the initials KKK carved in his chest. Hip, hip for Czechoslovakia. Of course, they don't have any blacks there. I wonder how they treat their Jews and Gypsies. I read a history of the area a few years back. Big religious conflict between Catholics and Protestants. Go back a little further, and they were burning heretics, like Jan Hus, at the stake. I don't think they're doing that kind of thing anymore. Be thankful for that. But history provides enough examples of people who struggled to achieve their freedom only to suppress freedom of others. Our Colonies for example. The only thing approaching freedom of religion was in Pennsylvania and Rhode Island, because they were governed by Quakers. If you were a professed atheist, you were in real trouble. Most of the Founding Fathers called themselves Deists—or Masons. I guess that was more acceptable—fashionable even. So . . . let's hear it for President Masaryk of Czechoslovakia. Maybe he has a brother or a cousin who could come over here and teach us a few things about championing liberty. Of course, he had better watch out where he speaks about such matters, or he might find himself hanging upside down in a tree with some letters carved on his chest—to teach him a lesson. To teach everyone a lesson. Words like that can appear to be so . . . un-American. So . . . unpatriotic.

Some white men broke into a student's room at Miles College and beat him up. Was it because they suspected he was a demonstrator or just to keep in practice wielding iron pipes? The same day, Governor Patterson ordered the expulsion of nine Alabama State University students who were involved in sit-ins. It didn't work this time. The next thing you know, 1,680 students marched in protest in downtown Montgomery. I heard that one in the news. They didn't say what happened. I heard about Tuskegee students starting a boycott of white businesses. Didn't hear what happened about that either. Maybe that inspired the Reverend Shuttlesworth to start talking about a similar boycott in Birmingham. It better be pretty big. If you try that with a few people, it's easy to arrest them and persuade them en route to prison not to try that again. This thing is beginning to snowball. Hard to keep the lid on things once they get started in earnest. These people are not intimidated anymore. They're not afraid to be messed with or beaten up. The old tactics are failing. I think things will get a whole lot worse before they start to get better. Aren't you glad you live over the mountains in a safe little suburb? Little chance you'll see any of the action up close. You do work in town, though. Downtown no less. Just keep your nose in your accounts and bring a brown bag lunch. And go out the back door at 5:00 PM to get to your car.

March 31, 1960

Dear Samuel,

Philadelphia. City of Brotherly Love. Ben Franklin's old stomping grounds, so I guess it's appropriate to hail Franklin for his words of wisdom: "Fear to do ill and you need fear nothing else." I guess the question remains as to what constitutes doing ill.

San Antonio became the first southern city to integrate its lunch counters. The Governor of Florida called that unfair and morally wrong. Everything is a question of perspective. I guess some people would consider carving letters in someone's chest morally correct—the activity of an upright, upstanding, right-thinking citizen. Got to keep blacks in their place. Let them munch on a BLT in the wrong place, and the whole fabric of society would unravel.

I'll be in Philadelphia for a while. A lot of historical sites to see—Independence Hall, the Liberty Bell, the site of the Continental Congress. Some of the streets have the same cobblestones they had back in the eighteenth century. At the same time, people tell me which neighborhoods are not safe to walk in, especially after dark. There are a lot of ethnic neighborhoods here—Polish, Ukrainian, Italian, German, Jewish. One of the people I met here grew up in South Philadelphia. He went to a school that was one-third Jewish, one-third Italian, and one-third black. He doesn't recall any major problems. No drugs, no turf battles, no violence. Then again, he moved when he was twelve. Maybe he was too naïve to notice. Maybe there was nothing much to notice. The kids played together in the schoolyard and out on the street—stick ball, wall ball, punch ball, step ball. There were no leagues. No teams. Just pick-up games. Whoever happened to be out at the time. No adults around to act as coaches. Maybe that was the key to the whole thing. No one around to teach you who not to let on your team. I think about that a lot. Is prejudice taught, or do we have a natural response to those we think of as being different? Then again, back then no one would have thought to let girls play with the boys. Later on, he said, when he was in middle school, religion was the big thing. The kids decided they had to get along with each other, so they started dialogues between Catholics, Protestants, and Jews. One of his friends, who happened to be black, got counted as a Protestant along with another friend who happened to be Japanese. Race wasn't a factor at all. One of his friends said his parents were against mixed marriages—they meant marriages between Catholics and Protestants. I don't think it would have mattered if the Protestant was as white as snow. He wound up eventually marrying a Protestant, but by that time no one seemed to mind at all.

I remember a passage from *Gulliver's Travels*. Swift writes about two religious conflicts—one between the right-footians and the left-footians and the other about the little-endians and the big-endians. The first conflict was about whether you should enter church with your right foot or your left foot. The king settled that argument by doing a broad jump and landing in the church with both feet at the same time. The second conflict involved which end of the egg you should open first. I don't remember how that got resolved . . . But when you figure how many people died fighting over the question of whether the bread and wine of the eucharist actually became the body and blood of Jesus or co-existed or were just symbolic representations. It seems that people have to attach their animosity to some supposed difference between US and THEM.

My humanist friend here throws up his hands and says, "Aren't we all human?" That's just the point. We are all human. Maybe that's where the problem lies. I think we share that characteristic with rats. They won't let a rat from another territory just march in and say, in effect, "I'm OK. Nothing to worry about." We are all part of the same species. We all have the same enemies. Sure. But you stay on your side of the barn, and we'll stay here. If you dare cross that line, don't be surprised if you're not welcomed with open paws, humans and rats. I'm not sure the rats would be flattered by the comparison.

April 7, 1960

Dear Samuel,

NYC. Getting restocked. The UN marks the Year of the Refugee—the plight of those exiled from their country of origin, either expelled or having fled out of fear for their lives. Does that include those forced to leave our beloved state out of intimidation or fear—the students that got expelled. The teachers that got fired—their families. Somehow I don't think that gets noticed at the UN. Too busy focusing in the Third World to see what's happening here. Our Ambassador to the UN can get filled with righteous indignation at what happens in Asia, Africa, or Latin America—not with what's happening in Alabama or Georgia.

Good old Dixie. Country of my birth. My childhood. Another country. It feels like I am in another country. Another world. I am an eternal tourist.

I remember a story I read in eighth grade—"The Man Without a Country." He had to stay on boats outside the country until the day he died. He turned out to be more patriotic than most. You never feel how much your native soil is a part of you until you are somewhere else. Thomas Wolfe wrote, "You can't go home again." I read that book in tenth grade. I can't say I remember too much about it beyond the title. I can't go home . . . yet. Maybe . . . someday.

How is my father doing? I bet he's on his high horse getting to show the nigrahs what for. Does he ever ask about me? Or does he think I'm a lost cause? A traitor. I won't try to imagine the language he might use. If you get a chance to speak with him, tell him I'm making good money as a salesman. Better money than I could make back home. Don't tell him anything more. He'll understand the money bit. If Yankees are willing to pay more for carpets than Southerners, why shouldn't I take advantage of that? You can even hint that I'm cheating them on what I charge. He'll like that. Let him think I'm getting over on gullible Yankees. He'd do it if he ever got the chance. He's sure any Southern boy could get over on any Yankee. So how did we manage to lose the War?

April 11, 1960

Dear Samuel,

I'm still in New York. The UN is celebrating the Economic Commission for Asia and the Far East. No Commission for Economic Development in the Deep South. But I've been over that territory before.

Well, a Civil Rights Bill somehow made it through in the Senate. They watered it down so it's symbolical at best. It's going to take more than that to accomplish anything. Maybe . . . Federal troops. The Civil War all over again. I hear that the Black establishment has just formed an Inter-Citizens Committee to focus on Civil Rights issues. That won't come to much of anything. They don't want to rock the boat. They are even more disturbed by what the students and the Rev. Shuttlesworth and company are doing than the white ones. The whites will promise them some token changes. They'll all talk about good will between the two communities, and the powers that be will sabotage even the few gestures that were made. It's going to take a lot more to bring about substantive changes. A lot more. And it won't be pleasant for anyone concerned—well, maybe for my father and his cronies. I wonder how often he launders his robe. Or does dried blood add to the mystique like notches on a gunslinger's six-shooter.

April 13, 1960

Dear Samuel,

In DC again. Seventh Annual Watershed Congress. I don't know what the issues are. I didn't know there were six other congresses before this one.

I wish I were still in NY. Did you see the bombshell in the *NY Times*? Front page article on Birmingham by a feature writer named Salisbury. Based on a visit to our fair city. Boy, if the locals knew what he was up to, he wouldn't have gotten out of the city alive. He discusses police brutality, false arrests, vigilante violence, bombings. He even managed to find out that the library banned a children's book because it showed black and white bunny rabbits that were friends. He wrote about radio stations' efforts to keep Negro music off the air. He made the citizens of Birmingham look like absolute idiots. Well, actions speak louder than words. Everything he wrote was true. Only he spent too little time in the city. He didn't get the half of it. Unfortunately, even half is more than enough. Who is going to move to Birmingham after reading that article? What doctor or professor would want to move his family to a town like that? How are the good folk of Birmingham responding? I bet they'll think it's libelous—based on Yankee stereotypes about the rednecks of Dixie. They'll be filled with righteous indignation—so they don't have to look at themselves in the mirror and respond to what they see. There's a buzz about the article in DC. After all, it was in the *NY Times*, and the *Times* is not known for yellow journalism. It might actually influence members of Congress. Even the President will have to respond one way or another. We shall see.

MAY 28, 1960

Dear Samuel,

I'm sorry I haven't written in a while. It's not as if things haven't been happening. I've been preoccupied. Cherchez la Femme. Isn't it always thus? I met her in DC at the Lincoln Monument. She was from Chicago—on vacation—to see the nation's Capital. She was standing there looking at the statue—intently. I made some kind of comment about how impressive the statue was. We got to talking. One thing led to another. I know DC pretty well. She let me guide her around town. Somewhere along the way, I told her I had never been to Chicago. She said turnabout was fair play. If I could be her guide in DC, she could be my guide in Chicago. As it turned out, I had planned to be in Chicago at the end of May. So . . . why not sooner? Why not, indeed? And she did show me Chicago, the obvious things—the art museum, the museum of science and technology—but other things a tourist would likely never get to see. What can I tell you? Things progressed rapidly from that point. She was intelligent, sensitive, personable . . . and very attractive. I think she found me intriguing as well. Even my Southern accent—not to mention my history. You live a while, you get to know what you look for in another person. I started fantasizing what it would be like to be with her a long time—maybe forever. And then I thought, what do I have to offer her? I'm a floater. OK, I sell carpets for a living. I could call myself a businessman. But sales is not quite a career. I don't see it as a career. It's just something I do. Could I make it a career if I settled down? Possibly. But can I see myself selling carpets for the rest of my life, not to mention the other stuff. I don't really have a career. I don't even have a sense of direction in my life. I suppose I could live just about anywhere. But I don't have any place I feel is really home or that I would want to call home. OK, if I'm with the right person, any place could be home. She really loves Chicago. For me Chicago is just a place I enjoyed for a while, especially being with her. And being with her was special. But how long could the relationship be the be-all and end-all of my life? That would put pressure on the relationship to be so great, it could make up for the lack of career, life direction, and a sense of home. And she wants to start a family. I can't see myself as a father—at least not yet. A father is supposed to teach his children what is important in life, and I haven't the foggiest notion about that. How could I explain that to her? She thinks that if the relationship is right, everything else will fall into place. Somehow I think that at least something needs to fall in place before I can ask someone to commit herself to a relationship with me. I said I needed some time to think about it. She said something about men fearing to make a commitment. I told her it wasn't the commitment to her that was the problem. I feel that I'm just skimming over the surface of life—completely rootless. The problem lay with me, not her. She didn't take that too kindly. She said she could see great things in me. I had real character. Values. She sees things in me I can't see in myself. Could I trust her vision? That was the problem. I have to feel well-grounded myself. I can't take that from someone else. I said I would play everything over in my mind. Think deeply about it—on the road. Get some perspective. But I don't think that distance and time will help. There is something missing in me. Some kind of psychic glue to hold the pieces together. I think it was Yeats who wrote about that in one of his poems. The center will not hold. Sometimes I feel that I have no center—that in the core of my being there is a void and all of my experiences can do nothing to fill it. Not even being with her. She is taking this as a failure on her part. I don't see it that way. The failure is mine. I feel like someone has offered to treat me to an elegant gourmet meal and somehow all my system can handle is junk food.

While all this was happening to me, the world was going about its business. The city of Birmingham filed a libel suit against the *NY Times* over the Salisbury article—and in a hurry-up trial, they were awarded some ridiculous amount of money, which I'm sure the *Times* will never pay. They printed a retraction about three minor points but stated that the rest of the article was accurate. I think that the libel committed was that the article didn't come close to describing just how terrible the situation really is. The suit claimed the article brought the city into public contempt, ridicule, and shame. Well, when you describe what passes for normal in the Magic City, what can you expect?

The stakes are getting higher every day. An activist black group was just formed in Raleigh, NC. Meanwhile a civil rights attorney's home was bombed. No one got hurt this time. It's getting nastier all the time.

Eisenhower signed the anemic Civil Rights Act of 1960. An all-white jury acquitted Martin Luther King Jr. of tax evasion. That was a surprise. It used to be that you could convict a black on just about any charge brought against him. If nothing else worked, you could always get him on a charge of vagrancy.

Did you know that the latest Civil Rights Act permits Federal judges to send referees to supervise voter registration? That will go over big in Birmingham.

May 31, 1960

Dear Samuel,

I'm back in NY. The U.S. postal service is celebrating SEATO—the South-East Asia Treaty Organization. An interesting collection of nations—the U.S., Australia, France, New Zealand, Pakistan, Britain, Thailand, and the Philippines. One doesn't usually think of the U.S., Britain, and France as being part of Southeast Asia, but I guess they have colonies there. I wonder, are they organizing for mutual protection, and against whom? China? Japan? Japan is now an ally but is not part of the organization. Pakistan, but not India. I really don't understand international politics. I can't say I understand national or even local politics either. I'm not sure that I want to. Everything seems to boil down to a question of power and money. People look you straight in the eye and then lie to you. Until they're caught. They don't seem to be apologetic at all. If everybody is doing it, why were they the only ones to be caught. It must be a plot cooked up by their enemies and therefore not based on fact. I remember an Attorney General who was jailed and tried to run for re-election from his cell. He still managed to get 40% of the vote. I think of the politics back home as being superlatively corrupt, and then I meet people from Illinois, Ohio, and New Jersey who tell me things are much worse where they live. So what is the answer? Move around from place to place so you never become aware of what is going on behind the scenes anywhere? Actually that is most probably what I am doing. I read a newspaper, glance at the national news, skip the local section. I'm still following the news from Birmingham. I guess I'm still attached emotionally to my place of birth. I want things to turn out for the best, even if I never get back again. It's like rooting for the home team that you know isn't very good. I met a guy from Philadelphia who was deep into baseball. At one point Philly had two teams, the Phillies and the Athletics. One year both teams finished in last place. Then in 1950, miracle of miracles, the Phillies won the pennant and played the Yankees in the World Series. They lost four straight. You kind of hope beyond hope that things will work out for the best. And then people do such bone-ass things, you figure they deserve everything they get. I'm not quite ready to say that. There are good people back home. But when good people stand by and watch bad things happen, evil takes over. There are a lot of evil people waiting to take over—pretty much everywhere. And they're the ones that make the news.

June 2, 1960

Dear Samuel,

Still in DC. The new stamp honors the women of America with a quote from the Bible: "She opens her mouth with wisdom and her tongue is the law of kindness." Nice words. Women have come into their own of late. They got the vote. Every once in a while they get elected into office. During the War they stepped up into jobs usually held by men—the men that were off fighting the Nazis and the Japanese. Once the War was over, the soldiers came back, and everyone expected the women to go back to the way things were. The same with blacks. They fought overseas to keep the world safe for democracy and then came back to Jim Crow. But if you feel like a man in France, you want to feel like a man in Alabama. And once you find out that you can hold your own putting rivets into planes and aircraft carriers, maybe you won't be satisfied anymore with just washing dishes, vacuuming the rug, and changing dirty diapers. I have the crazy idea that resistance to women's equality will outlast resistance to integration of the races. We like to think that our women are ladies, that they don't get their hands dirty doing things like science and engineering. And dishes and diapers—they're for the nannies to do. The nannies used to do everything—nurse the babies, keep the kids until they got to be ten or twelve. Then suddenly kids that were fishing together got separated overnight into masters and servants. Maybe that's why we're so neurotic. We got split off from our own childhoods. Except that in my case there were no nannies. And if my dad ever caught me fishing with a black boy, he would have at me with a switch so bad, I wouldn't be able to sit for a week. As far as women were concerned, they came in only two categories. The pure ones, you wound up marrying. The others, you lusted after. Maybe another reason we are sick in the head. Except I never bought into that. Show me a lady in a long dress with a hoop skirt, and I'm heading in the opposite direction. I like women who can get their hands dirty—maybe more than their hands. Women that can meet your gaze eye to eye without looking down or to one side. There are a lot of women like that up north and out west. We still hold on to supposed traditions that probably weren't even part of most people's lives. Maybe that's what they dreamed of—living the good life on a big plantation, having slaves to do all the work. I wonder what the slaves dreamed of.

June 10, 1960

Dear Samuel,

Well, here I am down south. Does Florida count as being southern? Parts, I guess. They say the Panhandle is about as Southern as it gets. But in Miami, life is anything but Southern. All these Yankee retirees that don't want to winter in the ice and snow anymore. All those Cubans coming up after Castro took over. The stamp of the hour says Let Freedom Ring. I'm not sure why that message would focus on Miami. Maybe there's a hidden message here. Wasn't it the Governor that said integration of lunch counters was immoral?

Walking through the Cuban quarter is an interesting experience. Cubans come in every color and shade. I'm sure if the darker ones tried eating at a lunch counter in Birmingham, they would be refused or arrested. What could they say? Pardon, señor, no hablo ingles. Would that get them a pass? Laws on the separation of the races don't apply if you speak Spanish and come from another country. And what do you do if you have to fill out an application and it asks for your race? Do you say Cuban and leave it at that? I've met other people from Latin America, and it's the same thing. Horrors! There must have been a lot of miscegenation going on. And the world didn't come to an end. I've met people from the Middle East. The same thing. Some look European, and some look African, and there's everything in between. Maybe it's just us that get upset at things like that. You talk to some people, and they think black people must be a different species. But different species don't interbreed and produce fertile young. The last I heard, Cubans and Arabs don't seem to have any fertility problems. Strangely, neither do white men and black women—or their children or grandchildren. The only difference is that we pretend the offspring are the race of the mother, not of the father. One drop of black blood is enough to condemn someone to second-class citizenship—unless the people are light enough to pass. Then they can move up north or out west, and no one will be the wiser for it—unless one of their children is a bit of a throwback. All this business about percentages—as if it really matters. If a truck is heading for you as you cross a street, do you want to check the percentage of the guy who rushes out and carries you to safety? Do you want to check the percentages of your doctor, your plumber, your florist, for God's sake. If they do something right, it must be the white blood in them. If they screw up or commit a crime, it must be the black blood coming out. Then you get people like my father. As far as I know, there's not a drop of black blood in him. If I had my druthers, I wouldn't want to eat at the same table with him. So much for percentages.

I am heading West again. It's warm in southern Florida. It will probably be warm all the way to Santa Fe. Hot. I saw the forecast. But I was born and raised in the South. Hot weather doesn't bother me. I like it hot. In more ways than one.

July 17, 1960

Dear Samuel,

I arrived here safely. The stamp commemorates the early Spanish settlement here in the Southwest. The Governor's Palace (yes, palace) was built in 1610. A bit of irony here. The Spanish came to exploit the natural resources here (what else is new!) and to convert the Indians to Catholicism. Back in the 1600s, the Spanish were not known to be a tolerant bunch. You were either Catholic, or you were going to Hell. I read a history of the early days. There was a Governor here who was called a Converso—a cryptic Jew. The Spanish ordered all the Jews out of Spain in 1492 (an easy date to remember). It was either conversion, exile, or death. Some people pretended to convert and practiced their old religion in secret. You couldn't do that. If they caught you, you could be burned at the stake. They did a lot of that during the Inquisition in Spain and Portugal. When the Spanish and Portuguese came to the New World, they brought the Inquisition with them. So when someone suspected the Governor of relapsing into his old ways, they arrested him and brought him to Mexico City for questioning. Three years of questioning. And questioning meant torture. Three years of questioning—three years of torture. That was considered an acceptable way to get a confession. I don't know why it would take three whole years to get someone to confess. Considering the methods they used, I think you could get a confession in three days—maybe three hours. The Spanish weren't terribly kind to Indians either. One account said that the practice of scalping was initiated by the Spanish and then copied by the Indians. The Indians did get something from the Spanish. They learned how to work in silver and a few more things like that. I'm not sure why we'd want to remember the Spanish settlements. We did everything to get the land from the Spanish, including initiating some very questionable wars. Everybody remembers the Alamo. Santa Ana is the great villain—killing all those valiant men defending what? We wanted the land. And aside from one small area we paid for, we took it. And we're not about to give it back. So hooray for Spanish culture—but New Mexico is part of the USA. End of story.

Interesting thing about the Inquisition. The Spanish felt they had to have a confession before they burned anyone. They didn't care how they got it, but they had to have it. In Alabama they don't worry about such niceties. I remember once they were after some young buck for making improper gestures to a white woman. Number one, it wasn't clear that he was even near the place he was supposed to have been near. Then they got the wrong man (it might have been a cousin). That didn't bother the lynch mob. One black man was as good as another. The point was made to the community in any case. Let Freedom Ring. Sorry, I'm not in Florida anymore.

There's supposed to be a First Day of Issue in Minneapolis tomorrow. Can't make that in time. A hole in your collection. After that, something is being issued in Birmingham. According to my sources, it will have three stamps, all of them previously issued before—the Statue of Liberty, Mt. Vernon, and the Santa Fe Commemorative. I can't figure that one out. I'll let you pick up the First Day of Issue. I won't be back in Birmingham for a while.

JULY 19, 1960

Dear Samuel,

It's been a month since I wrote last. I missed the stamps commemorating Hawaii's becoming a state. I can't drive to Honolulu. You'll have to get that one from a dealer. I've been spending my time visiting National Parks out West—making new business contacts, just enough to pay my way. Not a bad way to live. No house to worry about. No mortgage. No real estate taxes. Foot loose and fancy free, whatever that means. As long as my van holds out, and it's been doing pretty well so far. I just have to worry about gas, food, and lodging. I spend a few days hiking, hit a town, give my pitch to the local carpet outlet—and the local adult stores. Free as a bird on the wing. I meet interesting people. Swap stories. And then I'm on my way again. I had to make a choice. July 19 celebrated the one hundredth anniversary of the Pony Express. It went from St. Joseph, Missouri, to Sacramento, California, in eight days. The stamp will be issued in both cities at the same time. I chose to go to St. Joseph, so I headed back East. Beautiful country. It's a pity sometimes you have to put people in it. The first thing they do is mess up the landscape. I can't tell you how many pristine places I've been that are littered with our bottles and assorted trash. I've taken to bringing a large trash bag wherever I go. I can't get all the stuff out of lakes and streams. I feel like a custodian—a free-lance custodian, trying to clean up the whole country. People just don't give a damn about the natural world. Don't give a damn for the most part about each other.

What has been happening since I last wrote to you? Martin Luther King Jr. met with J. F. Kennedy. That's big. The NAACP is trying to get the injunction lifted that kept him from operating in Alabama. That's wild. The folks in Alabama think that's a radical organization. A Communist front. Amazing. They don't know what radical organizations are being formed that make the NAACP seem tame by comparison. I read a saying somewhere: "If you don't carry a deer today, you may be forced to carry an elephant tomorrow."

Then there is a court suit in Birmingham challenging separation in public facilities. That won't go very far. There is already a law about public facilities in interstate travel. No one in Birmingham pays much attention to it. At least not yet.

St. Joseph, Missouri, is north of Kansas City, right on the border with Kansas. Not much to write home about. I'm heading back East again.

AUGUST 12, 1960

Dear Samuel,

Arlington, Virginia. The tomb of the unknown soldier. I don't know why that gets to me. There is a person buried there. Nobody knows who he is. But he died fighting for his country. Every country seems to have a monument like this. If you're Head of State, one of the first things you have to do if you visit another country is to lay a wreath at the tomb of the unknown soldier. Someone lived. Someone died. Maybe in battle. Maybe in a latrine hit by a rocket. Hemingway has a novel about that. You get a medal for being wounded. It doesn't matter if you got wounded charging up a hill or sitting on the crapper. But what is the mystique about the unknown soldier? We all want to be remembered. We all want our names on a marker. Here lies so and so. He was a great husband and a great father. Or maybe not so great. But he was. He existed. And here is his name. So maybe his name isn't legible after two hundred years. Maybe eventually we all get to be unknown. Soldiers in the battle of life. But whoever the soldier was, he did live and he did die. One among hundreds that died without a name. That's the way it goes. There's a great war machine, and win or lose, there will be thousands that pay the ultimate price. For what? For the folly of leaders. Yours not to question why. Yours just to do and die. The story of mankind. The generals move markers on a map. Each marker represents a hundred or a thousand men. You win or you lose your objective. But in the meantime, a certain number of men will die. Pity. Now let's plan tomorrow's battle. It's like a football game. Only instead of being tackled, you get blown to bits.

I read an article about a group called the Black Muslims. They've given up on integration. They accept as fact that white hatred of blacks will go on forever. Let us get out of your hair. Give us some territory where we can set up our own state, and we won't bother you anymore. Where? They're talking about Black Belt, Mississippi. There are a lot of people who wouldn't mind. It's a poor area. Send the Indians to Oklahoma. Send the Blacks to Mississippi. Who cares?

Marcus Garvey wanted to take blacks back to Africa. We don't want you. You don't want us. A win-win situation.

But most Blacks have this weird notion that if they helped build the country, they should be a part of it. But the Black Muslims want to separate. They are true capitalists. They don't believe in buying anything on credit. Everything is cash on the line. They go into prisons and rehabilitate drug addicts and prostitutes. They get them to stop shooting up, smoking, drinking. No loud music. No gaudy clothes and gold chains and gold teeth. They set up farms and stores. They preach self-sufficiency. Marital fidelity. Hey, that doesn't sound too bad, does it? OK, they hate us as much as we hate them. But at least they're honest about it. I got a copy of their newspaper. They sell them on street corners—to Black people. But I got a copy anyway. Weird reading of history. As racist on their side as my father is on his. And they're not pacifists. No non-violent protests. Some of them are armed and know how to shoot. You've got to give people like that some level of respect. If the Klan wants to burn a cross on someone's lawn, if they want to beat somebody up or firebomb a house, they've got to know that they're not the only ones that carry shotguns. They've got to know that there's a price to be paid for everything you do. You go around shooting at people, you can get shot in the process. No free lunch. Eventually everyone gets what he deserves. Eventually. Maybe not today or tomorrow. But eventually. And even if you don't, you've got to live with yourself. That may be the worst punishment of all.

AUGUST 29, 1960

Dear Samuel,

I'm on the West Coast. Northwest. This is very different country. Seattle. The Fifth World Forestry Congress. I took the northern route this time. You'd think it would be cooler. It wasn't. The temperature in the Dakotas was in the upper '90s. It didn't bother me at all.

Crossing Washington State. The east part is rolling hills of grain and orchards. All based on irrigation and the selective damming of rivers. The central part is desert. Surprising to find desert this far North, but apparently the clouds hit the Cascades and drop all their rain to the West. Everything to the East of the mountains is arid, like the Southwest. Even the animals are similar. They've got diamond-back rattlers here just like in Arizona. You cross the Cascades, and it gets wet. Really wet. You have grey skies for days on end. The Olympia Peninsula is a veritable rain forest. Not many temperate rain forests in the world.

The people here are a bit schizoid. They love climbing mountains, camping out—being in the natural world—roughing it. At the same time, the logging industry is hot to chop down anything it can put a power saw to.

Most of the mountains here are potentially active volcanos. And the city of Seattle lies on a major fault line. I guess if you want a certain lifestyle, you have to be willing to pay for it somewhere down the line. If you want to live in Alabama. In Birmingham.

Things are heating up in my hometown. They arrested Shuttlesworth's kids in Gadsden for violating segregation ordinances in the Greyhound Bus Station. The Southern Christian Leadership Council held a worship service in a church in town. Attorneys are challenging the constitutionality of anti-trespass ordinances in the city. Students from up North are planning to come South to focus the nation's attention on discrimination in Dixie and to register Blacks to vote. Are you following all this, or are you just working in your garden? Eventually all this stuff will affect everyone whether they like it or not. I know that you're not a diehard segregationist or a rabid integrationist. You just want your life to limp along without too much trouble from either side. But eventually you will have to choose a side. At least if you want to remain in Birmingham. You could be like me and leave. Float free in the wind. Sometimes I regret the choice I made. But I'm trying to work things out in my mind. And I do get some perspective on things from a distance. I don't know what kind of perspective I'm forming or what I will do once that perspective becomes clear to me. If it ever does. But meanwhile I'm going through country that is breathtakingly beautiful. If I have to be in exile, this is not such a bad place to be.

October 24, 1960

Dear Samuel,

I'm back in NYC. Autumn. Beautiful. Not that autumn in Birmingham isn't beautiful. I'll say it about the city fathers (and mothers?). When they planned the city, they made a conscious effort to make it beautiful. They planted trees everywhere that blossomed in the springtime and turned every color of red and yellow in the fall. The Bradford pears. The red bud. The magnolias. The dogwood. The azaleas. If only this could have planned the social scene as well.

Instead of taking Salisbury's article to heart, the *Times* was sued for libel and ordered to pay a half million dollars in damages. The *Times* was ordered not to send any more reporters to Alabama. Talk about Freedom of the Press. What could they find out? That a Klansman rented a room overlooking Phillips High School and watched the school, high-powered rifle in hand, to make sure it wouldn't be integrated. That a minister was thrown out of the Methodist Congress and then reassigned to Southern Rhodesia for suggesting that his church be integrated. That a Bessemer court ordered Hughes to reveal the Alabama Council membership and financial records be made public—a court hearing packed with Klansmen shouting insults and threats that were not restrained by the presiding judge. That respected newsmen like David Brinkley, Chet Huntley, Edward R. Murrow, and Howard K. Smith (a Southerner) compared Birmingham to Moscow, South Africa, and Hitler's Germany. That the family of a student who won an art prize couldn't come to watch him receive the award because they were Black. That the poet John Ciardi was threatened, and the Unitarian Church that invited him to speak was threatened with firebombing, because he labeled Jim Crow as treason. So where is the libel?

What can I tell you? I watched the leaves turn color and fall. I read the *NY Times* faithfully every day. I imagine that the paper will appeal the judgment against it and will survive longer than its accuser. What does it take for someone to notice he has egg on his face—or even blood—without lashing out at those who notice and suggest it might be time to wash it clean.

The United Nations celebrates its fifteenth anniversary. Born on the ashes of the battlefields and the concentration camps of World War II—in an effort to further the cause of peace. In the world perhaps, but not yet in Birmingham. Birmingham, Moscow, Johannesburg. You don't need to be a professional journalist to make the connection.

November 2, 1960

Dear Samuel,

DC. The stamp honors another champion of liberty—Giuseppe Garibaldi, one of the heroes whose efforts led to the founding of the modern Italian nation. The George Washington of Italy as it were. Where is the George Washington that can be a champion of liberty in my hometown? Maybe we have such a champion. The only question is whether he will live long enough to do what needs to be done.

NOVEMBER 5, 1960

Dear Samuel,

Stamp issued in Vienna, Georgia, to celebrate Walter F. George's 34 years in the Senate (he died three years ago). Was his longevity due to his statesmanship or his kowtowing to the lowest common denominator of the electorate? God help me. I seem to see everything these days with jaundiced eyes. I'm becoming a real cynic. That's not good for me.

The leaves are falling. The trees are almost bare. If I were deep down in Dixie, winter would be forestalled for a while. The leaves would still be brightly colored. I am not in Vienna, Georgia, to get the First Day of Issue. If I were, I'm not sure I would have gone out of my way to acknowledge Senator George's service to Congress. Maybe yes, maybe no. You can get the commemorative issue from a dealer. I will hang out in the Northeast a bit longer. In Yankee country.

November 19, 1960

Dear Samuel,

NYC. Time to honor the words of Abraham Lincoln—not so popular down South after the Emancipation Proclamation freed the slaves. I just finished a book on that. He was ambivalent about Blacks. The Proclamation was as much a political tactic as a statement of principle. But he did say, "Those who deny freedom to others, deserve it not for themselves." That's pretty clear. I wonder how many of these stamps will sell in Birmingham. Hopefully the Post Office will deliver the letter—neither rain nor snow et al. But maybe ideology will keep them from their appointed rounds. Then again, postmen are Federal employees. They might even accidentally on purpose lose a letter with such a stamp on it. I'll hope for the best.

Sales continue good. I probably could open my own store here—maybe a chain of stores—for the carpets, if not for the other stuff. But something keeps me from settling down here. I don't want to get attached—rooted. I have the feeling deep in my soul that I'm waiting for something else to happen to give me a sense of direction. I haven't found it yet—or it hasn't found me. I feel like a leaf being blown about by an autumn wind, waiting to be buried in the approaching snow.

New President—JFK. News commentators say he squeaked his way in because of the Black vote in key states. I'm sure that makes some people delighted—and will renew efforts to increase voter registration in the South.

NOVEMBER 25, 1960

Dear Samuel,

Still in NYC. A stamp to honor the 125th anniversary of the birth of Andrew Carnegie—philanthropist and industrialist. I think they got it backwards. He was an industrialist first and became a philanthropist later. As an industrialist he took advantage of the absence of anti-monopoly regulations to exploit his workers and crush his competitors. He amassed a fortune and then decided to become a philanthropist. Do his acts of philanthropy erase the bloodthirsty tactics he used to gain power and riches? I read somewhere in the Bible that you couldn't use ill-gotten gains to offer sacrifices in the Temple. I wonder whether they ever used that criterion to judge the acts of donors—maybe three-fourths of the churches and charities in the U.S. might go bottoms up. The same people who swear up and down the line how kindly they treated their Negroes—in sickness and in health—as long as their Negroes slaved in the fields without complaint to provide them with the means to furnish their mansions with imported dining room suites and fine china and crystal. I went to a concert last week at Carnegie Hall. I saw a book there published by Carnegie-Mellon University. I guess the old boy did leave a legacy that benefitted society. I'm not sure his workers or his competitors would be so sanguine in their praise.

Have you been following the fortunes of Martin Luther King Jr.? He was arrested at a sit-in in an Atlanta department store. An earlier probation was revoked. He was put in a state prison, and two weeks later he was freed on bond after an intervention by the President's brother. It pays to have friends in high places. Maybe not quite friends. Allies might be a better term. The President doesn't want to appear to be on the side of the Yahoos. Not a politically wise move in these parts these days. What you can do to an ordinary person with impunity, you can't get away with someone in the public eye. Or the *NY Times* would shine a light on your escapades. Not that too many people in Georgia give a damn about that. They probably accept the fact that they are treated badly by the Northern press—that Yankees see them all as a bunch of rednecks. I've heard tell of people that proudly display signs in their cars—Redneck and proud of it. White trash, oil-field trash—what is the world coming to when a region of the country that has some heritage to be proud of defines itself by its lowest common denominator?

December 6, 1960

Dear Samuel,

I'm back in DC. I'm getting to know the road between NYC and DC like the palm of my hand. My van as well. It feels like I can just point the van in the right direction and the van will get me there all on its own. I can anticipate every curve in the road—every bump, every billboard, every pothole. Every carpet outlet along the way. Every adult shop. I'm a regular. They ask me how I'm doing. How's the family? I shrug and give some kind of nebulous answer. What am I supposed to say? My father is at a Klan meeting to plan how to respond to the Supreme Court decision that outlaws racial segregation on interstate buses, trains, and terminals, and he's feeling just fine. Swinging a mean lead pipe for a man his age. And the rest of them—it doesn't pay to even discuss it. I've gotten to the point where I can pretty well hide my Southern accent. People think I come from Indiana or Iowa or someplace like that. And I'm fine with that. I don't want to have to answer for the stuff that's happening in good ol' Dixie. I see how others respond to people with a Southern drawl. It's like they have some kind of venereal disease or leprosy. Well, I didn't choose where I was born and who my parents were. Can't help any of that.

The stamp honors John Foster Dulles, Secretary of State. Brilliant International Lawyer, Patriotic American, under the motto "Peace with Justice." I'm not sure the motto fits. He was one of the architects of the Cold War and, according to some people I've spoken with, a rabid anti-Semite to boot. Not that that was anything new in the State Department—which blocked an influx of Jewish refugees during and after the War. Pretty shameful what happened. Check on what happened to the ship the *St. Louis*, which wasn't allowed to let its passengers land in the U.S. and was sent back to Nazi-occupied Europe. We have a long history of prejudice against specific minority groups—the Chinese, the Japanese, the Irish, the Italians, not to mention the treatment of Blacks and Indians. I remember reading all that when I was in high school. I wondered why it wasn't in the standard high school history texts. What did they expect would happen when we found out what really occurred? It's enough to make one think of leaving the country, except that every country has a history similar to ours. All kinds of skeletons in the closet they'd prefer their young people not to find out about. Is that what it takes to be patriotic? Our country, right or wrong. Our country. Our race. Our class. Three cheers for the Red, White, and Blue. Help wanted. No Irish need apply. Our country club. No Blacks or Jews. Three cheers for our flag. Three cheers for John Foster Dulles. Brilliant international lawyer. Patriotic American. Sort of. Enough to get his face on a postage stamp. The true mark of success.

December 9, 1960

Dear Samuel,

The year draws to a close. I'm back in NY. Celebrating the International Bank for Reconstruction and Development. Unfortunate choice of words. Reconstruction. Boo. Hiss. Carpetbaggers and scalawags. Money for development in Asia and Africa, not yet for the Third World still present in the U.S.

December 15, 1960

Dear Samuel,

NASA is celebrating the launching of its first communication satellite. I'm not sure what that means. I'm not up on modern technology. People are saying it is the new revolution—as important as the invention of the printing press and the telephone. I suppose I will find out about what this means in due time.

This has been quite a year. I'll probably stay in NYC to bid farewell to 1960 and usher in 1961. I'm almost afraid to face the new year. Things don't look too good back home. I think they'll get worse before they'll get better. Whatever worse means, it will come to pass. People have to get dragged kicking and screaming into the future. If it worked for our grandparents, it should work for us. Slavery. Indentured servitude. Illiteracy. Bring it on. I'll make this short. Christmas is coming. A good season for sales. Let me tell you about my holiday line for stocking stuffers—a bit of holiday cheer on the nasty side. Maybe kill two birds with one stone. Do something wild on your next Romanian carpet. Something exotic. Oriental. Sexy. With your wife, your girlfriend—all your friends.

If I don't get back to you before, happy holidays. Best wishes for the New Year.

January 11, 1961

Dear Samuel,

I'm in Richmond, Virginia. About as far South as I'm willing to venture these days. Capital of the Confederacy. Ironically, the place where Patrick Henry uttered his unforgettable words before the Virginia House of Burgesses: "Give me Liberty or give me Death." A catchy slogan. Like the New Hampshire slogan—Live Free or Die. People always talk about dying for a cause. In the end most of them opt for life, whatever the conditions they're offered.

The Federal court just ordered the University of Georgia to desegregate. They will, of course, resist in some fashion. Maybe the Governor will symbolically stand in some doorway. Maybe some students or townies will show up with signs, bullhorns, stones, and bricks. But when push comes to shove, I don't think any of them will be willing to die for the freedom to maintain their prejudice. A few of them might be willing to kill—maybe some more to maim—but not to die. We'll see—once the troops arrive. And they will come. It's a new era. The South can call it the new War of Northern Aggression. But nobody's talking about secession. Gee. We may have made a little progress over the past hundred years.

JANUARY 13, 1961

Dear Samuel,

Buffalo. New stamp—15-cent airmail. Liberty for All. It looks like a propaganda war. All this talk about freedom and liberty on stamps—issued all over the country. People have to use stamps. At some level they have to look at them. Read the words. Subliminal propaganda. It takes a while to make the impact felt. Try to get two Black students into the University of Georgia. Two. Count them. One male and one female. I suppose, so they can date each other and not presume to cross racial lines. Two students. You'd think the Administration did something really radical and banned beer on campus. There were riots. The lily-livered administration suspended the two students. It would have made more sense to suspend the rioters, but that would be expecting too much. The courts ordered the two students to be reinstated, so I guess now they'll be taking courses like everybody else. It takes real guts to do what they're doing. I imagine they will get their share of insults—maybe worse. Somewhere along the line, their fellow students will figure out that the buildings won't collapse or sink into the ground and get back to what they're supposed to be doing—studying chemistry and math. Maybe philosophy and ethics. Maybe psychology. Look at themselves in the mirror and try to explain the supposed logic of their behavior. Ach! I am such an idealist. Such an optimist. Such a skeptic.

They're going to issue a stamp on Range Conservation early next month in Salt Lake City—conservation of natural and cultivated grazing land. Probably an appropriate place. The Mormons seemed to have figured out how to utilize land better than most for grazing and agriculture. I don't think I'll get out West. There's another stamp coming out in NY State the next day, and there's no way I can travel that distance in such a short time. The van is beginning to act up, and I can't push it the way I used to. I almost fell asleep at the wheel last night. I caught myself just as I was about to drive off the highway into a ditch. I have to get more sleep. I get to the end of a day, ask myself what I accomplished. It never seems like much. So I stay up reading or whatever. It doesn't seem to matter when I get to sleep. I always wake up early.

I'll be staying in NY State for a while. It's convenient. Profitable. I am beginning to meet people. Ah, you will say another woman. But it's not just women. People here get involved with news—with issues. I am this token white Southerner. They ask me how it really is down South and, in particular, in Birmingham. Is it really as bad as the news reports indicate? I tell them they don't know the half of it. I don't go into detail. They ask me why students would riot over the admission of two black students in Georgia. They all went to universities with Blacks, so integration at institutions of higher learning doesn't faze them. I ask them how many Black families live in their neighborhoods—if they know any of them by name, if they've invited them over for dinner, if they've been in their homes. If their kids hang out together. In all probability, if a few Blacks did move into their neighborhoods, real estate agents would try to create a panic in order to increase sales, and the neighborhood would be Black in a matter of months. They look at me and think I'm making apologies for the Deep South. OK, there are integrated neighborhoods in the North. But I know for a fact that there are also neighborhoods with covenant clauses that block selling houses to Blacks—some where you can't even have Black visitors. Where the response to integrating neighborhoods would look every bit as ugly as anything you could see at the University of Georgia. Well, maybe not quite as violent. No cross burnings. No lynchings. But there were race riots up North after the Black soldiers came back after World War I—after they fought to make the world safe for democracy. And I read a whole book on the Klan and politics in Indiana in the '20s. Some neighborhoods have gentlemen's agreements against selling to Jews—or Asians. Somehow that doesn't make it into the news. Which doesn't excuse the Yahoos from disgracing themselves in Georgia. It doesn't do any good to try to excuse yourself for acting like an idiot just because others are acting as stupidly as you are.

FEBRUARY 3, 1961

Dear Samuel,

Chautauqua, NY. Interesting name. Most probably Indian. The stamp honors Horace Greeley—American journalist and statesman, most well-known for his statement "Go west, young man, go west." And en route, encounter this or that Indian tribe, disregard their claim to rightful possession of the land. I suppose back then when he made that statement, the notion was that Indians were a mere impediment to our Manifest Destiny. If you read Hawthorne, the early Puritans seemed to have the idea that God placed Indians and virgin forests in America as a temptation—to get weak souls to take the safe course of sticking to the East Coast, where they had already handled the Indian situation one way or another. Indians were supposed to be living in a state of nature—savages. And since Nature was tainted by Original Sin, those ennobled by God's grace had to demonstrate their chosenness by getting rid of the Indians and the forests. The forests, after all, were a place where brute nature and uncontrollable impulses reigned, and of course you didn't want such impulses to win out over sober Christianity. And the only good Indian is a dead Indian. The only good buffalo, etc. The heritage we have to live with—that we have to live down. The Civil Rights Movement hasn't touched the Indian Question yet—probably by design. There are enough problems to deal with, and it's understandable that people would like to take care of their needs first. But eventually the movement as such to recognize that there are many groups left out of the American dream. I used to travel through some farm country in southern Alabama where migrant workers were used to harvest crops. The workers came in every shape and color. If anything, their situation was even worse than that of Blacks. No fixed place to live. No one checking living conditions. No minimal wage. No medical facilities. No schooling to speak of. You talk to the people. No hope for change. No leaders standing up for their rights. They are an invisible group to most people. You buy celery or plums at your local supermarket and have no awareness of how it was harvested. People want cheap produce.

That's how prices stay cheap. If consumers even had an inkling of the situation, it's not clear it would make any difference. People just don't care. There's no constituency here. They don't vote. As soon as the harvest is in, the workers go on down the road. You think about all the human misery in the world. On our very own doorstep. It just boggles the mind. It just boggles the mind.

FEBRUARY 13, 1961

Dear Samuel,

Back in NYC. The UN stamp honors the International Court of Justice in the Hague. What would happen if they investigated what is going on in the U.S. in my hometown—if they brought a few people back to answer charges? Crimes against humanity. We're not alone. Just about everything has a history it would prefer others not to look at too closely. There would be enough cases to last a century. What a Stygian stable! Is there any place in the world free of such injustice? And even if a few places like that existed, could someone go there in good conscience, knowing he had turned his back on all that suffering. I feel like a spectator watching a freight train careening out of control on a one-way track to disaster. I feel utterly helpless. And guilty. That's it. Guilt. It's almost overpowering.

MAY 10, 1961

Dear Samuel,

Council Grove, Kansas. The one hundredth anniversary of Kansas statehood. I haven't written in more than three months. I missed quite a few First Day Covers. Sorry about that. I have been . . . preoccupied. One of my clients. An adult store. A woman. You don't usually find a woman running an establishment like that. Most clients are men. Horny men. You wouldn't think they would accept a woman selling such stuff. It doesn't fit the fantasy. Then again, she could validate how the various devices really worked. Give testimonials. And surprisingly enough, there were a significant number of women patronizing the store. Call it women's liberation. Call it whatever you please. The store she ran had two sections—his and hers. And she was doing a bang-up business. As a side line—an adjunct to a medical section for people incapacitated by strokes, diabetes, high blood pressure. The more exotic stuff was in two back rooms.

We got to talking. She had her own predilections—tending toward S and M. Sadism and masochism. She gave me a few books to read on the subject. Psychology. History. Passage from the journals of Casanova about upper-class women being aroused at the sight of a rather gruesome public execution. References to the relationship between flagellation and arousal in men—especially in England, although the philosopher Rousseau seemed to be fixated on that as well. And of course, the Marquis de Sade—who seemed willing to be on either side of the lash.

I have to admit to you that the material was intriguing. A whole new territory—like suddenly discovering that right next door to you was an entire universe you were totally unaware of.

Well, here I am, wandering around the U.S., looking at this and that—an outsider, always looking at a window, watching people go about the business of living their lives. Somewhere along the way I would have to find some door to knock on—someplace to enter, to become an actor instead of a mere observer. OK, this is just an entertainment—fun and games, as it were. But you have to start somewhere. And I had nothing else better to occupy my time—at least for the moment. And I had a guide—an experienced guide to show me the ropes. She asked me whether I wanted to be the actor or the acted upon. Was I more interested in the sadistic or masochistic. It was all the same to her.

I had to think. Did I want to give pain or receive it? To be master or slave—or both and in which order, and how fast did I want to shift from one to the other. It's strange. I never thought much about my love life, as it were. Just let things happen. Go with the flow, with little reflection on what had occurred. Now she was asking me to think. To relate what I do to my image of who I am and who I want to be. This is producing some deep emotions. Disturbing emotions even. Do I see myself as someone who enjoys dominating others, or do I want to be dominated—to let others do what they want with me. Am I starting on a path leading to places I don't really want to go? Yet there is a fascination to tread in this unknown territory. Will I be able to return to whatever I used to call normal before, or will my life be irrevocably changed? I couldn't imagine doing this back home—although she assures me that there are more people into S and M down South than I could ever have imagined. Then again, considering the power trip people must have dominating Blacks, that might carry over into their sexual fantasies. Maybe some guilt as well. Emotions get very complicated. Sometimes opposite feelings lie right next to each other—or interfuse. The woman herself is ethnically, racially ambiguous. A woman of color—yes, but I can't tell where the color is coming from. Black, Indian, Asian—who knows. Maybe that adds something to the intrigue. So where do I go first? I guess being a white male, I didn't mind being dominant first. But it took some getting used to. She actually had to coach me on what to do. It felt initially more like a school experience than a spontaneous exercise, but she told me to have patience—the spontaneity would come. And it did. It was almost frightening how willing I was to subject another human being to my whims. My fantasies. I was frightened to admit that I even had such fantasies. I didn't take it very far. I was afraid to. What strange creatures we are. All that chaos lying just under the surface. A veneer of civilization holding all that chaos in check, and then if the situation is right, the chaos erupts. People vie with each other for front seats at a beheading or at a lynching. Secretly enjoying a crash at an auto race, a crunching tackle at a football game. Vicarious pleasures, dating back to Greek theatre—Greco-Roman boxing.

So here I had this willing subject to work on—or with—that was the difference. She was willing. She was more partner than victim. I think I liked it better that way—to know that she was getting some pleasure out of it, although I couldn't figure out why. How could anyone actually enjoy being tied up and whipped. Is there part of the female psyche that actually enjoys being dominated? Maybe part of the male psyche as well. I would find that out later.

I have to admit to you that there are times when you don't want reciprocity in your relationships. You want things to go your way, pure and simple. At the same time you want a real human being there—someone who responds, not just an inflatable doll or a dream image. What can I tell you without going into lurid detail? That I investigated a part of my psyche I didn't know existed. That it took my mind off . . . things—everything outside this small arena. For nearly three months I didn't read a newspaper. I didn't watch TV or listen to the radio. You could have told me the world was coming to an end, and I would have shrugged my shoulders and continued on with what I was doing. I felt like an explorer discovering a new part of the earth—terra incognita. All the while I wondered what she was getting out of this. Maybe she enjoyed being a teacher—a mentor. Maybe there was a part of her that really did enjoy being dominated. She never talked about her past. I never talked about mine. We were so engrossed in the moment, it was as if there was no past and no future. I could not have told you what day of the week it was or the date. Finally, I felt I had to step back and figure out what was going on with me. She was OK with that. Take a break, she said. When you come back, we'll switch roles. That felt like an invitation—and a threat. I knew her only as a passive recipient of my fantasies. I didn't know a thing about her fantasies and what to expect from her. I didn't know how I would respond to being acted on. And then again, I felt somewhat guilty being so preoccupied with my own emotions that I was out of touch with the rest of the world. While I was discovering my own emotions and gratifying them, the world was going about its business. And the business was none too pleasant.

The big news was the Freedom Riders leaving DC to bear witness to the Federal law banning segregation in interstate buses and terminals. I knew that would stir up a hornet's nest. I wondered if all those Northern idealists knew what they were getting into. A handful of young people confronting Southern mobs inflamed by the latest affront to their way of life. I suppose when you're young, you can throw all caution to the wind—or maybe believe that the ultimate goodness of mankind will prevail, that they had the ability somehow to change hearts and minds by appealing to man's better nature. Except those redneck types don't have a better nature. They are what they are, and they're proud of it. So there.

So here I am in Kansas wending my way back to NY. I'm listening to birds singing. Looking at sunsets and sunrises. And damn. I know what's going to happen. I just know it as certainly as I know what will happen if I throw a bottle in the air. It will come crashing down to earth. It will shatter on the concrete—break into a million pieces. And people walking barefoot will cut their feet on the glass slivers. And they will bleed.

June 5, 1961

Dear Samuel,

I'm back in NYC. I feel like Jeremiah crying in the wilderness. Like Cassandra, prophesying accurately to anyone and everyone she meets. But no one will listen to me. The news about the Freedom Riders is everywhere. Pictures of the burned bus in Anniston. The beatings in Birmingham. The arrests in Jackson. The Attorney General sends in Federal marshals, but in truth doesn't want to get involved. He expects local authorities to do what they are pledged not to do, which is to enforce the law as interpreted by the Federal courts. Where will all this end? The Bull is firmly entrenched in power—thanks to the mandate given to him by the white citizenry. He is in league with the Klan—or at the very least with an organized mob of irate lowlifes. The police arrive on the scene conveniently after the Riders are beaten to a pulp. And meanwhile the city leaders still hope to attract doctors and scientists and their families to Birmingham to build a medical center with an international reputation. We have an international reputation founded—images of drunken Yahoos beating unarmed young people while the police stand by and do nothing to prevent or stop the carnage. If you were a doctor from Chicago or Seattle, would you want to go to a place like this—bring your children? OK, you might buy a house over the mountains—far enough away so as not to hear the shouts and the screams. But you'd still have to work in town. Maybe you could gaze into your microscope so intently, you wouldn't notice anything. Maybe you could ignore the separate restrooms and fountains. The separation of patients. Maybe you would specialize in dealing with blunt-edge traumas.

I hear that the U.S. Department of Justice is talking with Civil Rights groups about beginning Voter Education Projects, whatever that means. Some of the groups are starting voter registration drives in Mississippi. That would be something, wouldn't it—to think that Mississippi would forge ahead of Alabama in an area of basic citizen's rights.

Meanwhile the stamp honors Dag Hammarskjold, who was killed in a plane crash. He never visited Alabama. Might not have gotten out of there alive even without a plane crash. They held a memorial service at the UN. Impressive. A choir sang Beethoven's Ninth Symphony—the text was based on a poem by the German writer Schiller. I don't suppose that would go over big back home, unless they kept the words in German so no one would understand. Alle Menschen werden Brüder. All men are brothers. Or rather will become brothers. Not yet. Not in our neck of the woods.

June 28, 1961

Dear Samuel,

I sent you a few envelopes from here and there. An eleven-cent stamp of the Statue of Liberty with the words "In God We Trust." Today's issue from NYC—the Liberty Bell with the words "Let Freedom Ring." Is this some subtle message about what is going on in Birmingham? If so, the subtlety is going unnoticed by folks like my father, who, if he had to post a letter, wouldn't bother to notice the message or connect it with his actions. In God We Trust. Sure. The Bible, which justifies segregation as part of the divine order. The curse of Ham—for all eternity. That clearly justifies Black subservience to the white man. Don't plant diverse seeds in the same field. Don't interbreed two species of animals. And isn't it clear that the Blackman is a different species from the White? What God has separated, let no man join together. QED. Maybe the message of the stamps is meant to be ironic. Who runs the postal service anyway? Who determines what stamps are to be issued and what to say?

Meanwhile there is an even-handed order from a U.S. District Court. The judge orders the Freedom Riders not to demonstrate in Alabama and bans interference by the Klan. The ruling is contested by the U.S. Department of Justice and the NAACP. There are no stamps to honor the Freedom Riders who were beaten in Birmingham. No stamps yet to honor those that beat them. I guess that would be called even-handed.

July 11, 1961

Dear Samuel,

I am in DC. The new stamp honors the hundredth anniversary of George W. Norris—Distinguished Statesman. Senator from Nebraska. I'll have to do some research on the man. I'll confess I never heard of him before. Either he wasn't all that distinguished, or I am totally ignorant of those worthy of being honored. Strange that the stamp would be issued in DC rather than in Nebraska.

Things are happening too fast for me to process them. I keep looking at the pictures of the bus in Anniston. All the pictures of the bloodied faces in Birmingham. Worse is the image of the faces of those wielding the pipes and bludgeons. I keep looking for my father's face. I haven't found him yet, but I did recognize some of the other faces. Good churchgoers, all. I have to get away from all this. I don't want to watch TV. I don't want to read the newspapers. I don't want to know what is going on. I know what is going on. I know what will happen tomorrow.

October 4, 1961

Dear Samuel,

I have not written for a while. I took a break. Remember the invitation to investigate the other half of S and M. Well, I did. I let myself be tied up and whipped. A bit more than that. The woman is a real expert. It's not just that she knows what toys are available and how to use them. She knows how to get her partner involved. It was hard for me to acknowledge that I could be aroused by dominating another person. But to be aroused somehow by playing victim, that was new for me. She stretched out the sessions, prolonging the agony, as it were. Leading me step by step into more and more exotic situations. She was not only the initiator. She was the educator—the guru. She gave me passages to read—mostly by the Marquis de Sade and Sacher Masoch. We were not only to be involved with the sensual activity but with a philosophic enterprise as well. The freedom of submission—without losing any sense of personal integrity or character. One can come to a realization that it is part of human nature to be the tormentor and the tormented—to have the power of life and death over someone or to be at someone's mercy. It is precisely when one overcomes the fear of death that one can face life squarely. Maybe that is the secret of what is happening in Birmingham—except that the tormentors don't accept the possibility that they could be vulnerable and the persecuted can't accept even the possibility that they could persecute others. That is why the drama drags on. We don't recognize the humanity of the other or of ourselves. The possibility of being both tormentor and tormented and receiving some sort of gratification from either role. So I got a taste of both. I wonder if I am the better for it.

The new stamp issued in DC honors Frederic Remington—Famous American Artist (and Sculptor) and Illustrator. He celebrates Western America. The arena of cowboys and Indians. I will give him credit where credit is due. He ennobles both sides. His Indians are not savages—semi-human monsters. They are just who they are—

expert horsemen. Hunters. People, no more or less than the settlers that displaced them as the dominant population.

Where are we headed? New rules prohibiting discrimination in interstate bus travel are supposed to go into effect in about a month. I thought they were supposed to have gone into effect six years ago. New voter registration drives in Mississippi—at least one activist is killed in the process. I suppose that all revolutions must have their martyrs. A Federal Judge ordered that 67 parks, 38 playgrounds, 8 swimming pools, and 6 golf courses run by the city must be integrated by the first of the year. I wonder what Bull will do about that. He certainly won't let it happen without a struggle. I mean, come on. You can't let Blacks picnic or swim alongside Whites. The earth might be thrown out of orbit. And play golf together. Horrors. Tennis. Mixed doubles. Indeed.

October 10, 1961

Dear Samuel,

I'm still in DC. The stamp honors the fiftieth anniversary of the Republic of China and its leader Sun Yat-sin. I'm not sure why. Another hero of freedom in some distant part of the world. Maybe next year a stamp honoring the Freedom Riders. Hardly.

OCTOBER 24, 1961

Dear Samuel,

NYC stamp honoring the UN Economic Commission for Africa. So we can help improve the economic situation of Blacks halfway around the world. Not yet those in Blackbelt, Alabama; and Mississippi. Am I off-base, but is there something crazy in all of us? I ran across someone from South Africa—actually two people, one White and one Black. Apartheid is law in South Africa—de facto and de jure. There was a prominent American Black that visited South Africa as an official delegate of some program. They couldn't discriminate against him without creating an international furor. The way the White explained it, apartheid only affects native Africans, not Blacks from abroad. The attitude toward native Blacks is akin to our attitude toward Native Americans. So there is no contradiction affording equal treatment for a foreign Black—as long, I suppose, as he dressed like a European or American dignitary and came with a sign or badge identifying him as a foreigner. Not that certain white south Africans wouldn't be outraged. Maybe like Huck Finn's father when he saw a well-dressed Northern Blackman strutting around for his ninety days of freedom, before he could be subjected to capture and shipped back down to the South as a slave. The Blackman told me that a few native Blacks took advantage of the practice by dressing up like European or American tourists or dignitaries. Although that was gutsy, since their accent would give them away. Similar to what happened in south Louisiana. I wrote to you about that before. The older I get, the crazier everything seems to get. There may be a logic to it, but it is a logic I would prefer not to understand.

November 6, 1961

Dear Samuel,

Springfield, Mass. A stamp honoring Dr. James Naismith, the inventor of basketball. Interesting problem. Up North the teams are integrated. But the Northern teams when they come south—like college teams, the professionals—what to do? They can't play in places like Birmingham. They can't stay at the same hotels. They can't eat at the same restaurants. They can't use the same buses. Remember what happened when Jackie Robinson first played for the Dodgers—the insults. The death threats he received. And now that there are other Blacks playing pro ball. Maybe that's why we can't see pro-ball down South—at least not at the level of the Majors. There it is. You want to see baseball at its best, adapt. If not, be satisfied with semi-pro, segregated teams. How long before that barrier falls? Maybe a compromise. Pro-ball. Integrated play but separated fountains and bathrooms. Separate bleachers for the fans. We are a clever people. We can figure something out. Give the fans something to cheer about. The bankers something to celebrate.

I heard a joke about a football game with a black halfback. He broke a tackle and raced toward the end zone for what would be the winning score. A white man jumped up, cheered, and shouted, "Look at that Injun run."

New demonstrations targeting the bus terminal in Albany, Georgia. I don't know the town. Is it anything like Birmingham? If so, God help the demonstrators.

November 7, 1961

Dear Samuel,

NYC. Stamp honoring General Pershing—American military leader who died thirteen years ago. Is that how long you have to wait to be honored? Do you have to die first? It would be nice to be recognized for something you did while you were still alive. At best, like Dag Hammerskjold, just after you die. Make your family happy. Your friends. People imagine you looking down from the Heavens smiling that you were being so honored for having lived—not that half the people honored on stamps are truly remembered. When I was a kid and dabbled in stamp collecting, collecting baseball cards, and such, I collected all kinds of things—it was the collecting that mattered. We cared more for a card that was rumored to be rare than for the person on the card. There were no pro-baseball teams in Birmingham. We didn't really have a home team to root for. If a card was rare, we didn't care what team he played for or even what league. It was the same with stamps. All we cared about was filling the page with stamps. It didn't matter what the stamps depicted. Most people are lucky to have fifteen minutes of fame. More, if what they do is infamous. I imagine people will remember Bull Conner for much longer than the people working to defeat him—the great criminals longer than the people that brought them down. Hitler, Stalin, Mussolini, Genghis Khan. I run on a bit. I had better stop before I get myself depressed.

I pick up a newspaper. Front page article features a normal family with normal children that go to church every Sunday, get good grades, and help old ladies cross the street. Sure. Maybe on page 37 under the ad for lingerie.

January 6, 1962

Dear Samuel,

A new year. I am out West again. Beautiful country. Celebrating the fiftieth anniversary of the 47th and 48th states to join the Union. How's your history? Can you name the states? Clue, I'm here in Santa Fe. I will probably journey over to Phoenix early next month. Mild winters around here. No wonder older people move here for their retirement. Pretty mild winters in Birmingham as well. But you can't enjoy the city parks. Bull Connor closed all public recreation centers rather than see them be integrated. Ain't that a pisser! I wonder what percentage of the people back him on this. I'm not sure he gives a damn. He has his constituency. Even if he lost it, they don't call him Bull for nothing. Don't invite him into your china shop if you expect anything to remain unshattered. He's not alone. Circuit Judge Walker B. Jones issued a permanent injunction against the NAACP in Alabama. If he thinks those guys are so radical, he should notice who's coming up behind. A local court ordered the seizure of Abernathy's and Shuttlesworth's cars to pay off a libel suit. Amazing. It's like they're using fly swatters to chase off a herd of elephants. A herd of elephants that once sufficiently incited might set off a rampage.

Albany, Georgia, is turning out to be a flashpoint. Arrests of students for walking into white sections of the bus station. Arrests of Freedom Riders from Atlanta leading to mass demonstrations and mass arrests—over 500 according to news reports. Enough of a flashpoint to attract King to Albany. I think he went there specifically to get arrested. And so he was. Serious charges against him—obstructing a sidewalk and parading without permit. I guess they could have charged him with vagrancy as well if they wanted to.

The mayor apparently wanted to avoid a brouhaha, so he's postponing King's trial for sixty days—a cooling off period, a tactic to take people's minds off the incident, so when the trial finally comes, no one will notice. Not everyone is as heavy-handed as Bull Connor. There are some white boys who are clever enough to defuse the situation with chicanery rather than lead pipes and two-by-fours. An elegant chess game. You want to win, you have to have a good strategy. Good opening moves, a good middle game, and certainly a good end game. A way of detecting your opponent's weakness and then going for the throat . . . politely, civilly, so no one can accuse you of being boorish. Not like Bull, who can sense the game is going poorly and just upsets the board, hoping no one will remember where the pieces were. A master can play many games at once and keep his strategy clear in every game—like a Commander-in-Chief of the Armed Forces, fighting a military campaign on many fronts at the same time. And let's face it. This is a war on many fronts. I'm not sure who the Commander-in-Chief is on either side. There may be more than two sides. That makes things really complex. A bunch of little commanders each thinking his skirmish could be the decisive one in the war. Except I think the tide has already begun to turn. It's just that few people in the field realize it. Like the Battle of Chalmette. The battle was fought after the War of 1812 was actually over. Tell that to the soldiers that died there only to find out posthumously that their deaths were meaningless. Ah, well.

February 16, 1962

Dear Samuel,

Phoenix. I've been visiting national parks. Almost deserted in the winter time. Not bad to be alone sometimes—to collect my thoughts. Experience a bit of Nature in the raw. People make a great deal of fuss over their little ego games. In the natural world, the individual doesn't count for much. I remember an evening back home some years ago. Swarms of insects flying everywhere, especially around lights. They looked like mosquitoes, but they didn't bite. I asked someone about it. It turned out they were just about all males—millions of them. Every once in a while, a female. The drama of the individual mosquito came to little enough. By morning, there were piles of them lying dead on the ground. Only a very few got to fulfil their destiny and pass their genes on to the next generation, and I took out several females that were trying to sample my blood. I thought of people—millions trying to achieve an unconscious goal, some instinctive drive to allow the species to be perpetuated for another generation. Except that unlike mosquitoes, if our species suddenly disappeared from the earth, I think Nature would continue on its merry way without missing a step. A few centuries and there would be few enough signs of our presence on the earth. And with it all, we strut around on the world stage as if each of us really mattered—our wishes, our prejudices, our loves, and our hates.

You take someone like Bull Connor. There is a tide coming. His efforts to put up a dam of sticks and mud will go down in history as a pretty futile effort. Of course for the ones who die in the effort, for them the obstruction is devastating. For them and the children they never had. Maybe for those so traumatized that they become dysfunctional or so embittered that they will disaffect others in turn. But there will come a time when the obstruction will be swept away—when Bull Connor will become the smallest footnote in a history book. And if Bull Connor, all the more my father and his kind. Just a small footnote in a weighty tome.

So Bull Connor closed all the parks and recreation centers to stop them from being integrated. And now the movement to re-open the facilities has begun. Timidly to be sure. The over-the-mountain folk can't match the brute power of the Bull face to face. Eventually, though, they will get tired of his antics and find some polite way of getting rid of him. Not by brute force, but some clever backroom strategy.

Meanwhile, the unrest spreads. Southern University in Baton Rouge—the largest state university for Blacks—has been shut down. They tried expelling a few students for taking part in a sit-in demonstration. A few years ago, the event would have passed without media notice. This time the campus exploded. The students wouldn't accept this act passively. They acted in concert. I don't know what eventually happened—whether the expelled students were reinstated. But the balance of power has clearly shifted. And if in Baton Rouge, then in other places as well.

You can pick off a few rebels, one cluster at a time. But when all the clusters join together, all the Black organizations that once were at odds with each other—SNCC, CORE, the NAACP (now the Council of Federated Organizations all working, for example, on voter registration)—there will be changes in the offing. Bull Connor be damned.

February 26, 1962

Dear Samuel,

Back in NYC. The UN celebrates a Commission on Housing and Community Facilities, again in the Third World. The last I heard, segregation in housing was alive and well all over the South—and many suburban areas of the North as well. You restrict people to the worst areas of the city and then wonder why their children don't turn out well. Poor housing, poor jobs, poor schools. Three strikes and you're out. There are precedents for all this. They call the areas ghettos—originally a term used to describe the Jewish quarters around Europe. Somehow in spite of everything, the Jews managed to survive, even prosper. The will to survive. The question is how to encourage such a will to survive in our black ghettos. Some people make it to the top in spite of everything they're subjected to. They make it out. But where the only viable option is to make it *out*, what is left is an increasingly dire and pessimistic situation. Even that may be changing. The stores in the black neighborhoods are generally owned by whites. The goods they sell are generally of poorer quality, the prices inflated, the interest rates high. The personnel are usually not drawn from the community. There are the unremitting marks of segregation—separate changing rooms, bathrooms, water fountains, lunch counters. The sit-ins haven't accomplished much yet. The tactics are changing. The community is being encouraged to boycott stores that won't change their policies. That seemed too subversive according to the authorities. They arrested a few organizers, Shuttlesworth among them. It's amazing the fortitude that man has. So you change the words a bit. No boycotts. Just selective buying. Turn the divide-and-conquer strategy on the store owners. Pick them off one at a time. Money talks. Hey, listen to me. I could be a community organizer. Except I'm no longer part of the community. If I showed up with a plan like that, I'd be regarded with suspicion by blacks and be called a traitor to my race by whites. In NYC I can pass as just another person whose opinions are no more or less noteworthy than those of countless others you might meet walking on the street. I can theorize all I want—it doesn't come to anything. The real actors are far from here. Their heads are on the chopping blocks. And before it is all over, some of them will die.

April 11, 1962

Dear Samuel,

It's a great chess game. Blacks threaten a selective buying campaign. Connor counters by threatening to cut funds for 70,000 in the Black community. One could appreciate the game more if people's health and very existence were not at stake. The pressure to change the status quo increases. The ACMHR petitions to have all the racial signs and job barriers removed. Blacks file for public office in Jefferson County. The HIC petitions downtown stores to have them desegregate. SNCC workers stage sit-ins at the Attorney General's office to protest arrests in Baton Rouge. Step one. The Mayor tosses the ACMHR petition in the trash. The Democratic committee disqualifies all the Black candidates. Shuttlesworth is arrested again, this time for obstructing a sidewalk. Counter move to the counter move. Federal Judge Grooms orders the Black candidates to be put back on the ballot. Some Blacks stop patronizing white-owned stores. The selective buying campaign is selectively successful. Meanwhile the U.S. Supreme Court rules that both interstate and intrastate transportation facilities must be integrated. And the Defense Department orders full racial integration of all military units—except the National Guard. How would you score the game at this point? I think the inregrationists are pulling ahead, but the contest is far from over—except for Roman Duckworth, who is shot to death by a cop in Taylorsville, Mississippi. For him the contest is over. It doesn't matter who is ahead at this point or who will eventually win.

The funny thing about death is that it is final. You don't get to see how things play out after you're gone. Martyrdom seems like a noble act—in passing. But with your passing, all the accolades and monuments don't help you one bit. I wouldn't mind being injured, maimed, crippled even—just as long as I could acknowledge in some sense the recognition for what I had done, or even to acknowledge it to myself. The grave's a peaceful place, but none there do embrace or something to that effect. I read that somewhere back when. I was never good at memorizing lines of poetry. I actually have started jotting down notes to remember even what happened yesterday. My memory is getting a bit iffy these days. Maybe it's a sign of aging. The first signs of incipient dementia. That would be a pisser, wouldn't it? To be on the road, alone, far from home and not to remember where I am, where I'm going, and why. I'm not sure I know why even at this point. Will I become a basket case—be carted home where people will take care of me? Who would take care of me? My father and his kin would see me as a pariah. They might decide to do me in—slip something in my food and say I died of natural causes—or be a bit more blunt. Do me in with an axe and dump my body in the woods—say I just wandered off and had gotten lost. No one would know any better. No one would care one way or the other. And that's saying something for a person my age. No wife. No children. No significant other. Just passing relationships that didn't come to much. Nothing that I do counts for much. Selling carpets that are an imitation of the real thing. A good imitation, possibly, but an imitation nonetheless. And the sex toys. What can I say? The French have an expression for this (they always do)—a nouveau frisson. The latest thrill. A new titillation—to ward off boredom. Because in essence there's no real relationship there—just a few new sensations. And repetition is deadly. Is there in fact nothing new under the sun? Maybe relationship—a real person to interact with? No. Anything but that. Give me that vibrator. That new lotion. Give me something. Anything. OK. Here. Some new stuff. Straight from Europe or the Orient, where the act of sensuality is a real art. Enshrined in Temples and quasi-religious texts. As long as we're in the real world, we need to understand it—experience it in all its permutations, even if ultimately it is all illusion. So I am a Purveyor of illusions. The illusion of relationship. And I, not even the illusion of relationship. Everything passagère. Passing. Nothing sticks. I am in eternal limbo. Waiting for something to happen I can label as significant. Knowing that the real drama is back home. Maybe . . . years ago. When I was born. At such a cost. My very existence, such a cost. Like Oedipus. Only would that it have been my father that had died. Not her.

Charles Evans Hughes. Jurist and Statesman. Chief Justice of the Supreme Court. A reflection of the ultimate court. The heavenly court. Maybe . . . my whole life . . . to make up for what I did at birth. And I have not come close. Not even close.

April 25, 1962

Dear Samuel,

Cross country again. Seattle. The Space Needle. Century 21 Exposition. It doesn't matter how far I go. I don't think I will make it to the 21st century. Not that it will matter one way or the other. Be that as it may, the Space Needle is impressive. Being that Seattle is right on a major fault line, I'm not sure it would remain standing if a big earthquake happened here. They get small tremors in Seattle about six times a year. People take it all in stride. When it's your time to go, it's your time to go. I don't think we have any major fault lines in Birmingham. Then again, we are in tornado alley. People who don't live in Alabama don't realize this. They think tornadoes only happen in places like Kansas and Nebraska. But we do have tornadoes. A lot of them. And violent thunderstorms. And of course we do have Bull Connor and his crew. The locals are beginning to realize what this means. You sent me the article in the *Birmingham News*. Front page. The impact of the boycott. The impact of world opinion concerning our fair city. People don't really want to face facts. Don't go to the doctor. He might tell you that you have a serious disease. Cancer. Just let the tumor grow and spread. Pretend it's not there. Cover your eyes and think nobody can see you. We used to do that as children. When children do it, it's funny. We all laugh. When adults do it, it stops being funny. Cancer isn't funny. It eats you up inside. A lot of things can eat you up inside. And then you die. Hopefully without too much pain. Mask the pain with opiates. Walk around like a zombie and call it living. I'm still alive. Sort of. The city is still alive as well. Bull is still alive. My father is still alive. My mother is dead. I killed her years ago. The price for my own existence, such as it is. She got the short end of the stick. Who knows what she would have been able to accomplish if . . . if only? It boggles the mind. Boggles. The mind. My mind. I mind. Time to head East again. Southeast. New Orleans. The 150th anniversary of Louisiana's entry into the U.S. OK, they left during the Civil War and were forced back. And they're playing the same game as Alabama nearly 120 years later. I'll let you get that First Day cover from the dealer. A river boat. Ol' Man River. Must know something, don't say nothing.

I'm headed for NYC again. Time to resupply again. I'll travel through the Badlands of the Dakotas. Rough country. Insidious. I have a whole month to make it. I almost said home. Back to NYC. Back. Maybe one day. Not yet.

MAY 25, 1962

Dear Samuel,

NYC. The UN stamp. To live together in Peace with each other. Sounds good. The folks back home will tell you they were living together in peace and harmony until outside agitators began to stir things up. Black folk were happy with their station in life. They were taken care of by people who were concerned with their welfare—as long as they didn't rock the boat. And if they did, well, it wouldn't take too much to convince them to stop.

They are not stopping now. Six of the black candidates were elected in the Jefferson County Executive Committee. Has the boat overturned yet?

George Wallace won the Democratic nomination for Governor. That means he will be the next Governor. That should be interesting. Not exactly a progressive force on racial issues. At least not for some. It looks to be a long hot summer.

JULY 24, 1962

Dear Samuel,

It has been a while since I last wrote. Another interlude, as it were. I think it goes with the territory. I sell adult toys. I attract people with more exotic tastes. Of late, it seems to focus on S and M. People enjoy dominating other people, or they want to be dominated, at least in a protected way, in a game-type situation—role-playing. Always time to step back when things start to get scary. Step back and have a drink. Sack out. Start again the next morning. Things getting a bit more radical. More than just binding and flagellation. I'm not sure you want me to go into detail. Call it a process of discovery—just how far I'm willing to go to submit another person to pain and suffering, even if she enjoys it. How far I am willing to submit myself to her. Can I trust that she won't go too far. Interesting that after the role reversals are over, there is a sense of camaraderie—appreciation that the other person was willing to play the game, a sense of mutual trust. The interaction almost approaches what I might term relationship. Almost, but not quite. Somehow the game has limits. At a certain point it is a relief to step back. To hit the road again.

Burlington, Vermont. The stamp celebrates the fiftieth anniversary of the Girl Scouts of America. No merit badges for what I've just been through. I met someone from Philadelphia whose father was involved with the Cub Scouts. The father led an integrated cub scout troop. The Boy Scouts started pressuring him to transfer his black members to a black troop so all the kids could be more comfortable being with their own kind. The Boy Scouts. In Philadelphia. Not Birmingham. Things are more subtle up North, but it comes to the same thing. Maybe we could reach a point of subtlety in the South. Would that be an improvement? At least down South you know exactly where you stand.

The University of Virginia graduated its first black student. Voter registration drives continue in Mississippi—in small towns. Demonstrations after the arrest of students who participated in sit-ins and other demonstrations. A federal judge issues a permanent injunction against Birmingham's bus segregation. A division of U.S. Steel in Tennessee has begun a gradual desegregation of its 20,000-person workforce.

Things are gaining momentum. My father must be going crazy. My father. His cronies. The Bull. The Klan. I ran away from home when I was fifteen. I'm still running. Crosses are still burning. My stomach burning. A lot more of late. Nothing some antacids can't handle. A few. Blue. Pink. I think. That's the problem. The strongest chain. The weakest link. I think I need . . . a drink.

July 28, 1962

Dear Samuel,

Down the road apiece. Norwalk, Conn. To honor James O'Brian McMahon—U.S. Senator. Father of U.S. national nuclear policy. I'm not sure what the policy entails. Maybe dropping a bomb on Birmingham to calm the strife. It worked in Hiroshima and Nagasaki. You show you mean business, and they back down. The bombs ended the war with Japan. OK, they killed over 100,000 people and left many more with radiation-related diseases. Would the world be a better place if Birmingham were wiped off the face of the earth?

OK, there are some good people in Birmingham. Would a just government kill the good with the bad? If there are fifty righteous people in Birmingham, could it be saved? How about 45 . . . 40 . . . 30 . . . 20? How about ten? And then, if the city were saved, what of the majority who are evil? Where is justice to be found in this world? The good suffer, and the evil seem triumphant. I don't suppose that has changed much over the centuries. What is the significance of such a state in the world? Do I even have an inkling, an iota of understanding—a note or scintilla, a speck, an atom? If I did, would that enable me to go home again? Not roam over the face of the earth nibbling at games of torture to get at the part of myself who, when all is said and done, can enjoy seeing others suffer. No justification needed. I like it. I really do. And maybe feel guilty at the same time. The need to harm. The need to feel guilty. To do penance. To suffer in my turn at the hands of someone more adept than I. Penance. Atonement. Is there ever absolution? Forgiveness? Salvation? Is that what I am seeking? Waiting for? Some eternal state of consciousness. Beneficence. Peace. I should live so long.

AUGUST 31, 1961

Dear Samuel,

DC. The 25th anniversary of the National Apprentice Act. I'm not sure what that is supposed to do. Most kids need a college degree these days to get anywhere in the world. It's not like it used to be a century or two ago, where just about every trade required a period of apprenticeship. Certain people back home are not considered acceptable either in college or apprenticeship situations unless they stay with their own kind, mostly in underfunded, inferior institutions. A Federal judge ordered Montgomery to integrate its libraries and museums. Level the playing field a bit. Maybe the powers that be will close the libraries and museums. That would certainly level the playing field. Turn a whole generation of kids into ignoramuses. And in the process, keep the Northern and world press from focusing on Birmingham—throw some minor concessions at the black community in an exchange for a cessation of public demonstrations by either Whites or Blacks. It won't work any which way. Maybe for the establishment Blacks or for the business community. But an increasing number of Blacks aren't satisfied with tidbits and crumbs anymore. They have developed a taste for prime steak. The Yahoos don't want the Blacks to have even one crumb. One crumb. Stay dumb. Stay numb. Bite your tongue. Pull out a plum. By gum. In sum, Tweedle-Dee and Tweedle-Dum. Ho hum. Dark rum. I'll have some if you don't mind. A double shot. Drink it neat. Can't be beat. Can't stand anymore on my own two feet. I think I'm being a bit incoherent at this point. What's the point of coherence when nothing much makes any sense anymore. Can one make sense of lunacy? Folie à deux. Everyone is mad. Some foam at the mouth. Others go about their business quietly. I'm the Emperor Napoleon. Treat me with the respect that is my due. Moo. Get out of my way. It's time for me to gorge with the other bovines until I recognize the ultimate sovereignty of . . . what? I don't know. I don't know anything anymore. Nothing at all.

September 16, 1962

Dear Samuel,

The new stamp honors Sam Rayburn of Texas—Speaker of the House of Representatives. Leader of the majority Democrats. He was just shy of 80 years when he died. Four score. The Bible speaks of three score years and ten. Anything after that is a decline. But Moses took over leadership at eighty and continued on for another forty years, just shy of the Promised Land. OK, Sam Rayburn was not quite Moses. Didn't get us even close to the Promised Land. You can get that First Day cover from a dealer. I'll be in NYC. They're honoring Dag Hammerskjold again. It must be nice to be famous enough to get honored twice. No honor among thieves. Talladega passed an ordinance outlawing demonstrations and picketing. Two churches involved in training people to increase voter registration of Blacks are firebombed in Georgia. What do you think of that, Mr. Rayburn? Oh, so sorry. You're dead. How about you, Mr. Hammerskjold? Oh, you're dead too. That's the easy way out. The coward's way. How are things in Bonham, Texas, Mr. Rayburn? Any demonstrations or picketing?

Things are quiet in NYC. Sex toys are selling like hotcakes. Orgasms aplenty. Better individual orgasms than social paroxysms. I am doing well. If you haven't heard, there's a sexual revolution going on. Come, join the fun. Whites over here. Blacks over yonder. Separate restrooms. Separate fountains. Separate dildos. Separate but equal. Definitely equal. Nerve endings. Erogenous zones. Do Blacks, being decidedly more primitive, have more fun? There's a PhD thesis topic for some enterprising soul. Dance and sing on the plantation—in front of their shacks—while we watch from the veranda, mint juleps in hand, and enjoy their insouciance. I like that word. Insouciance. Got to punish them for their insouciance. Boy, look at them dance.

October 24, 1962

Dear Samuel,

Here's a good one. A stamp honoring the UN's efforts to maintain peace in the Congo. That's somewhere in central Africa. The Belgians got out. They left a mess. Things degenerated into tribal warfare. Power struggles between men and their followers that didn't give a damn how many people suffered and died as long as they got to live high off the hog. The Belgians don't care what happens anymore. They're safely back in Belgium. Meanwhile, thanks to the UN, a few Dutch people go over and help a few Africans learn how to drive tractors. Does anything make any sense anymore? Hey, UN people, how about some more tractors for Birmingham. Oh, sorry, that's an internal question to be solved by the Congress and the President. Too bad, Mr. Rayburn. He dead.

SCLS convention in Birmingham last month. It was covered by some international papers. Downtown stores had all the racially exclusive signs removed. As soon as the reporters left, Connor had the signs back in place. When the cats are away, the rats will play. Merchants that even pretended to give an inch on segregation policies suddenly got hit with new fees and fines for supposed violations of the fire code and such. Martin Luther King says he plans to integrate the University of Alabama. Hopefully he'll do better than similar efforts at the University of Mississippi. It took Federal Marshalls to escort James Meredith through the registration process. Whites rioted in protest. A foreign newsman got killed. That's what happens when you enter a war zone—in the Congo. In Mississippi. Can Alabama be far behind? We are never far behind. Just as long as Mississippi is last in everything, we don't mind being 49th or 48th. We look at places like the Congo and nod complacently. Chaos in the Congo. What do you expect from a bunch of savages? Self-rule. A joke. Blacks can't even hold their families together. How do you expect them to run a country? As well as we can. He, he, he. It takes civilized folks to run a country. Civilized white folks, like Bull Connor, don't you see? Civilized folks like you and me.

NOVEMBER 1, 1962

Dear Samuel,

Season's greetings from Pittsburgh. A little early, but what the heck. Get your shopping done early. Only I have no one to shop for. More's the pity. I do have gifts others can purchase. Buy your honey a carpet. Genuine imitation Persian carpet from Romania. Might be better than the original. The weavers in the Middle East are almost all Moslems. They have this idea that only Allah is perfect. So if they're nearing the end of the weaving and the work looks perfect, they'll consciously put in a few irregularities to make a theological point. I don't think the Romanians have such a theology. So they tend to weave a perfect rug. So you can tell the original from the imitation by checking for irregularities. The rugs with the irregularities are worth much more than those that are perfect.

Don't have enough for a rug? Buy your sweetie a dildo. They came in all colors and sizes. Let her indulge herself. There is a risk. She may come to value the imitation over the real thing—especially if the dildo vibrates. If you can buy it early, I can have it gift wrapped. Don't worry. I have toys she can buy for you as well. All kinds of toys. Even S and M. As you approach the Lenten season, a little suffering will get you in the holiday spirit. That is, if we make it to the holidays.

Cuban missile crisis. Playing chicken. Who will back down first? Monroe Doctrine. We can't have the Soviets build missile sites 90 miles from Florida. Will we take the sites out with nuclear weapons? Will the Soviets retaliate in kind? Nothing to worry about. There's nothing of strategic military significance in Birmingham. Although the Soviets might decide to bomb a hick town just to make a point. We did that kind of stuff to Germany at the end of the War—just to show them we could. I'm not sure Hiroshima and Nagasaki were of any military significance. So maybe it's time to check out your bomb shelter. I don't have to worry. Pittsburgh is a long way from Cuba. OK, it does have some steel mills. But I'll be on the road shortly, riding through the hills of Pennsylvania. Waiting for all this nonsense to blow over.

Oops. Missed the news. The crisis is over. Kennedy faced down the Soviets, and they backed off. Good practice. Now can he face down Governor Wallace and Bull Connor? Now that's a real challenge.

November 14, 1962

Dear Samuel,

Back in DC. The stamp honors Justin Smith Morrill. You remember him. He first formulated the Land Grant Act—a hundred years ago. That led to the founding of many of the state universities. Not a bad policy. You give the government land of no mineral or agriculture value, get some kind of tax write-off, and the state gets to build on the land. In Dixie you need twice the land grants so you can build separate White and Black universities. Separate and theoretically equal, although everybody can see through the ruse. Mediocre faculty for the Blacks. Then you can point to the graduates, notice how inferior they are, and talk about the genetics of human intelligence. OK, there may be a few exceptions. A Blackman is selected as Attorney General in Massachusetts. A congressman in California. Oh, those bleeding heart liberals. But also a state senator in Georgia. In Georgia. Wow. But a few exceptions don't disprove the generalization. The exception probably had a few White genes kicking around. Theme of the tragic mulatto. Reaching for new heights, constantly being pulled down by inherent savagery and sensuality. We should create special neighborhoods for such people. We wouldn't want them in our neighborhoods. No telling when the Black genes would manifest themselves. And even if they didn't, we wouldn't want to give the wrong message to our children. Whatever the wrong message might be.

There will be a stamp issued in Chantilly, Virginia. I'm not sure why. Nothing special. Just a regular eight-cent airmail stamp. I'll pass on that. You can get it from your dealer. I'll be heading West again—to Springfield, Illinois. You can imagine why. A postcard honoring Lincoln. The great war to preserve the Union. Are we in fact one nation? Or two? Two sets of laws. The Feds can legislate whatever they want. Enforcement is another matter. Lincoln is probably turning over in his grave, assuming that some kind of consciousness extended beyond death. Maybe oblivion is to be desired. Something to aspire to. I am more than halfway there.

November 23, 1962

Dear Samuel,

Less controversial. A stamp honoring Washington. Father of our Country. Slave owner. Jefferson as well. They made compromises to get the Southern colonies to join the Union. Still paying for that. The year is coming to a close. Is that cause for optimism? For hope? Sales are good. I will be able to maintain myself in exile for the foreseeable future. Drag my bones through another year. To what end? Is mere survival sufficient? Prospects of aging. Wandering around until I can wander no longer. I will wind up in some unknown town—destitute. In a nameless pauper's grave. Well, death is death. Better a living jackal than a dead lion. I don't know how long I can continue like this. The holidays approach. All that shlock about being home for the holidays—about the true meaning of Christmas. Joy to the world. I don't see much joy these days, except for people who market this or that to put under the tree. Which, I guess, inspires me. Give your honey a dildo under the mistletoe. Worth a kiss or two. Oh, darling. Just what I wanted. You know me so well. You do. Let's return to the bedroom and do a little celebrating on our new carpet. It looks Persian. And looks are everything.

December 3, 1962

Dear Samuel,

NYC. The UN building. I think they could finance all the expenses of the UN just from the sales of stamps alone. New issue commemorating the Commission for the Peaceful Use of Outer Space. Not many settlements in outer space yet. Maybe some satellites. I guess they could put weapons on board. Hard to defend against stuff coming in from outer space. Except that once a potential enemy develops some sophisticated weapon, their enemies will develop some kind of anti-weapon system. It keeps on going like that. The only people who win at this game are the companies that produce the stuff. So we keep on developing more and more intricate weapon systems. The Soviets as well. And meanwhile in the Congo . . . While in Birmingham they use pipes and clubs. I guess that says something about our civilization. And what differentiates a developed country from a primitive one—the kind of technology people use to kill each other. A pleasant thought as we approach the holiday that is dedicated to the "birth of the Prince of Peace." Sure. How many atrocities perpetrated in the name of the Prince of Peace. I remember they used to plan lynchings for Sunday afternoon after church—a picnic on the grass. Make sure the men were off from work and the kids were out of school. Don't want anyone to miss the fun.

DECEMBER 5, 1962

Dear Samuel,

DC. Honoring Sir George Cayley—father of aerial navigation. I don't understand. He died in 1857. What kind of aerial navigation was he the father of—hot air balloons? With a name like that, he must have been English. What were the English doing back then to advance progress in aerial navigation? Nothing that I am aware of. Then again, I'm not exactly a student of history. I suppose I could look it up in some specialized encyclopedia if I were really interested in finding out—which I'm not. I'm not interested in much these days. I'm just floating along. I look up, and weeks have passed me by. I don't want to study history. I don't want to know what's happening in the world. Well, maybe something.

A change in the charter of the city of Birmingham. The most important thing is that Bull Connor's office will no longer exist. Clever. They couldn't get rid of him in a general election. No chance of impeaching him. I wonder who the clever soul was that figured this out. I may have underestimated the intelligence of at least one of the city leaders, such as they are. I wonder if Bull is entitled to a pension for the time he served. A small price to pay. I don't imagine he will go quietly. Who the Hell cares as long as he is gone. Let out to pasture. He used to broadcast baseball games. I suppose he could go back to that without creating too much havoc. Maybe he would use the format to air his views.

Hello. This is Bull Connor about to announce the play-by-play account of this game. But first a comment on what your Federal government is doing for you—or rather what it is trying to do to you, against you. The President just signed an Executive Order banning discrimination in the sale or rental of Federally funded housing. He signed an Executive Order because he was too chicken shit to try to get the damned proposal through Congress. So there it is, folks. The President is telling you who you can sell your homes to. What next? He will soon be telling you who you can live with. Freedom in this country of ours is going down the tubes—going to Hell in a bucket. It's time to get organized. The niggers get together for their sit-ins and whatnot. It's time to show them that White folk can also get organized. There is going to be Hell to pay. These muckamucks think they can get over on us Southern boys, but they never had to face off against a redneck with his dander up. You just wait and see what is going to happen. You want to be part of the action? There will be a sign-up sheet after the game. Don't worry about whether the Feds find out if you're on the list. We'll keep it quiet. Besides, if the niggers have the freedom to sit in wherever they please, it's legal for us to do what we have to do. Sauce for the goose, sauce for the gander. Now, here are the starting lineups for today's games. For the visitors, playing shortstop and batting first . . . That's the way it will go. Bull Connor, sportscaster. You can't keep a good man down.

Gloucester, Massachusetts. Kennedy country. Pretty country, although this time of year it gets pretty bleak. The year winds to a close. It has been quite a year. I try to take my mind off things. The stamp honors a painter—Winslow Homer. He liked painting seascapes, especially in stormy weather. I suppose it's nice to watch storms at sea from the safety of a cliff overlooking the ocean. Like me watching the storms blowing over Birmingham from the safety of Glouchester, Mass. You see a boat in trouble from the safety of the shore. Not much you can do about it except marvel at the height of the waves. Will the boat make it to shore or get torn apart and sink under the waves. Will the city survive? Probably. But in what kind of shape? Who knows?

JANUARY 9, 1963

Dear Samuel,

New Year. I spent the occasion quietly enough alone with my own thoughts. It's essential to be able to find pleasure in one's own company. I watched the ball drop in Times Square on TV to the music of Guy Lombardo and the Royal Canadians. All those people shouting with joy as the New Year was ushered in. The image of Old Father Time handing over the reins to a baby—with infinite potential as it were. For good, supposedly, but also for evil. Image of people hugging each other. Dancing. All the people in the ballroom seemed White. The orchestra as well. In Times Square the people are all massed together—White, Black, and probably every ethnic, national, religious, racial, and social group under the sun. It doesn't matter who you bump into. Who you talk to. Everybody is celebrating. So . . . I too celebrated. A bit of eggnog laced with a bit of rum. And then a bit more. I sipped it slowly to appreciate all the flavor. The nutmeg. I really enjoy nutmeg. And the rum. Dark rum. I'm not sure when I fell asleep. The TV was still on. A news station. I turned it off. I didn't want to hear any news just yet. And then I turned it on again. The Rose Bowl Parade. Float after float made up of flowers. Nature in the service of mankind. In the service of beauty. Sweet young things waving to the adoring crowds. And then the game. The Rose Bowl itself. People hanging on to each play. Cheering for their side. White and blacks playing on both teams. Well, the teams were from the Big Ten and the Pacific West Conference, not from the Deep South. The game was played in California, not in Alabama. For one day I could let myself go. And I did. A bit more eggnog with a bit more rum. I felt just fine. Let a few more days pass before reality seeps in. Or maybe doesn't seep in. Flow in. Surge in like a tidal wave. The U.S. Justice Department sues segregated school districts in Alabama, Mississippi, and Louisiana that serve Federal installations. A classic confrontation of States' rights vs. Federal jurisdiction. Happy New Year.

The stamp shows the first U.S. flag—thirteen stars and stripes representing the first thirteen colonies, including some from the Deep South. The United States of America. Not so united then or now. I am . . . afraid. More afraid than I ever have been before. The fear grips me every waking hour. It invades my dreams. I wake up in the middle of the night in a cold sweat. There is a passage from the Bible I remember. The curse that threatens the people of Israel if they don't obey the Divine laws given to them. During the day they will hope for night to fall—for the agonies to be over. At night they will pray for the dawn. And hunger will beset them. Such a hunger that they will eat their own children. An image by the Spanish painter Goya of one of the gods eating his own child. Terrifying. It is early in the year. Already I am praying for the year to be over. I don't want to face what the year will portend. I want to cover up my eyes and plug my ears with wax. I want to curl up in a ball and sleep like Rip Van Winkle and wake up in twenty years to a new world so different, it will take me weeks to understand it—a time when the image of Times Square will be the norm, not just on New Year's Eve in Times Square. Not just with thousands of people anonymously jostling against each other but really relating to each other. Twenty years. Will that be enough time? Will I have to live through every agonizing day, every hour, to get there? A spectator. Watching from afar as the real actors go through the motions. Oedipus kills his father. Marries his mother. Puts his eyes out. Orestes kills his mother and her lover to avenge their killing of his father. Hamlet as well, I watch from afar. Watch them die so I can live—I, who wish his father were gone from the scene. I, who killed his own mother so that I could live. If you call what I am doing living. Writing to you. So that you can bear witness to my suffering—from afar. And be able to do nothing to save me from my fate. It is only January 9. I want to sleep. Oblivion would be a blessing. Hamlet contemplates suicide. All that holds him back is the fear that after death there will be no oblivion. That he will be cursed with consciousness for an eternity.

FEBRUARY 4, 1963

Dear Samuel,

NYC. Conference on Science and Technology in Geneva, Switzerland. A pastoral setting for dealing with industrial progress. Progress. The vain optimism that somehow science and technology will usher in an era of social felicity. We have been here before. The early 20th century. The hope. The optimism. And then the dashing of all hopes as the new technology was used in war. Now you could kill your enemy from afar. You could drop bombs on his cities from airplanes and dirigibles. You could wipe out hundreds at a time with poison gas. The horrors got magnified. Industrialism was dehumanizing workers. Turning them into cogs of a great machine. And the artists went about idealizing primitivism. The noble savage all over again—except he was truly savage. His claim to fame was that he killed his enemies with an axe, not a bomb. Artists indulging in the creative powers of the unconscious mind, where, as Sophocles noted, every man kills his father and marries his mother. The heart of darkness. Who know what horrors pass through the minds of women?

The drama begins to unfold. The modern tragedy. The new city charter is upheld in court. Theoretically Bull Connor is gone. But he holds on to his powers pending a decision by the Alabama Supreme Court. I daresay if the decision were to be handed down by the U.S. Supreme Court, he would ignore it completely—like Governor Wallace in his inaugural speech, calling for segregation now, segregation tomorrow, and segregation forever. Meanwhile the Federal Court overturns the convictions of demonstrators convicted of disturbing the peace. The battle lines are drawn. The first shots have been fired. Who knows what carnage lies ahead?

March 22, 1963

Dear Samuel,

I have not written. Seven weeks. I . . . have been busy. Selling. More selling. Demonstrating the efficacy of my wares. Demonstrating. You'd be surprised how many people want proof before they buy anything. Watch how my stain remover takes out the stains in your rug. The gravy. The wine. The blood. Watch how this gadget can tickle your fancy. Give you sensations you never imagined were possible. No end to the possibilities. A lot of demonstrations. Sit-ins. Lie-ins. I have been very busy. The UN issues a stamp. Freedom from hunger. Two-thirds of the world's population is underfed. The image is of a white worker feeding a black child. The White man's burden. We create the problem. We have to fix it. Where is this black child? In the Congo? In Canton, Mississippi? Who is the white man who is feeding the child? The white woman? Will they be shot for the work they are doing? The same day a stamp is issued honoring Andrew Jackson—a great warrior before he became President. Not quite a hero for Indians. The only good Indian is a dead Indian—or at the very least, an Indian on a reservation, a pitiful stretch of land that cannot support the impoverished native Americans we force to live thereon. No whites handing out food for those folks. We created the problem. We make no effort to fix it.

The Alabama Supreme Court upholds the permanent ban on the NAACP. An appeal to the U.S. Supreme Court will most probably overturn that ruling, and in turn that ruling will be ignored. Two Blackmen win spots in a run-off election for the Birmingham City Council. That's interesting. I wonder if they are the accommodating sort, willing to accept crumbs from the table, or those that want chunks of meat and whole scoops of mashed potatoes and gravy.

I'm sorry this letter is so brief. I have other demonstrations to give today. Other demonstrations. Other lie-ins.

April 6, 1963

Dear Samuel,

Hey! Bull Connor is defeated in his bid to become Mayor of Birmingham. That's a relief. Maybe people are finally coming to their senses. I'm not too familiar with the guy who won. Is he better than Connor? How is he likely to respond to the on-going demonstrations? The on-going demands. Change often comes from the top. If he is willing to change, change could come more quickly—more peacefully. Then again, people like my father would be incensed. They don't exactly respect authority. Any authority. As long as dynamite is readily available, there's no telling what will happen. You remember reading Huck Finn? It was one of the books we weren't supposed to read. That was a good one. We got a hold of the list of forbidden books and made it a point to read every one of them. I probably wouldn't have read half of them if they hadn't been on the list. I would have missed out on the better part of my education. Remember the part where Huck's father sees the well-dressed Negro walking about the streets of the town. He knows the man has some weeks of freedom before he can be seized and returned to slavery. And he is ticked off. The nerve of a nigger parading up and about dressed like that—pretending to be better than white folks, even the poor white trash like Huck's father. A pity my father never got to read Huck Finn. He wouldn't have understood it even if he read it. He wouldn't have wanted to accept the message the author intended even if he understood it.

I met a man like that a few years back—in Indianapolis. He seemed educated. His neighborhood was beginning to be integrated in nibbles around the edges. I asked him if he would mind if a black family moved next door to him. He said yes. I asked him why. He talked about criminals and drug dealers. I asked him if he would mind if the family included a doctor and a teacher. He said yes. I asked him why. He said that if the family were like that, his children would probably befriend their children and want to associate with them—visit each other's houses and so on, and that would never do. I didn't pursue the matter further. But there's the problem. It's not just Yahoos like my father that are impeding the process, not just people who hide behind white sheets and burn crosses. At least they're honest about their feelings. The guy in Indianapolis would probably object to being called a racist or bigot. He's just an ordinary bloke. A moderate even. A lot of moderation like that back home, God help us. Probably just as many up North if truth be told. They just hide their true feelings better. What can I tell you.

The stamp is interesting—the 300th anniversary of the Carolina Charter granted by King Charles II of England. Interesting. Settlers petitioning the King of England for the right to settle in this new land. Where exactly did the King of England get the right to grant that land to anybody? Didn't it belong to the natives of the land? Oh, sorry. They didn't count. Their claim to the land they lived on for centuries didn't count. That pattern repeated around the world. A bit nervy, wouldn't you say? Like walking into a store and claiming a piece of jewelry for your own without compensation to the owner. I think there is a word for that—Theft. And the last I heard, an injunction against theft is part of the Ten Commandments. Interesting how we pick and choose which part of the Bible we follow.

April 26, 1963

Dear Samuel,

Surprise—I went down to North Carolina a few weeks back. What was I thinking? Was I homesick for Dixie? Perhaps. I'm back in NYC again. The new UN stamp—an airmail postcard. I'd have to write really small to fit everything in. And there's a lot to write about. Things are heating up in Alabama and Mississippi. The NAACP announces a campaign to end segregation in Jackson, Miss. They also file a petition on behalf of Blacks who want to enroll in the University of Alabama. Governor Wallace promises to block that effort. One of the Freedom Riders is murdered in Keener, Alabama, by a grocer from Gadsden. The marchers continue on. Someone arrested. I'm not sure what the charge is—maybe vagrancy or parading without a permit. Martin Luther King is arrested in Birmingham. He smuggles out a letter, which is released to the Press, criticizing white clergy who are against his campaign. Easter Sunday. Blacks do a kneel-in in some white churches. Heavens to Betsy. The very idea that Black Christians could want to celebrate the Resurrection in the same church with Whites. What would Jesus have said about such nerve? A prayer meeting at City Hall. I'm running out of space. Can you read my tiny script. I'll continue in a bit in a letter. More space.

MAY 3, 1963

Dear Samuel,

Silver Spring, Maryland. A commemorative for the life of Montgomery Blair—Postmaster General under Lincoln, who pushed for a Universal Postal Union. I suppose that was a good thing. I tend to think of Maryland as being Northern—or at least in the middle, but there have been riots in Maryland over the question of integration. I can't keep up with the news from our neck of the woods.

A state circuit court in Alabama bans parades, pickets, sit-ins as a breach of the peace. Not the bombings and beatings. Just the demonstrations. Protestors arrested en masse for trespassing. Whites avoid stores that are being picketed. So I guess that tactic is working. Some locals are branding all such activities as being instigated by New York Commie Jews. It figures. King and his associate are freed from jail. I'm not sure why and how. Others are kept in custody. Their arrests are being appealed on grounds of freedom of speech and assembly. I guess Alabama thinks those Constitutional rights were guaranteed only to Whites. Blacks didn't constitute full humanity back then, so the Bill of Rights was iffy for them at best. I hear that Blacks are going to use high school students in their demonstrations. A bold move. Clever. I don't think the authorities could come down hard on children. It would look really bad in the national press. Then again the police and the authorities don't seem to care how they are seen by the press outside the South. They seem to accept the fact that Yankees and the rest of the world portray them as moronic bigots. They play victim to the world even as they beat, firebomb, and lynch their fellow citizens.

Here's a good one. Got that in a small article in a local newspaper. The Secretary of CORE was held in contempt of court by a judge in Gadsden because she wouldn't respond to being addressed by her first name. She refused to post bail. The case is being appealed to the Supreme Court. The nerve of such people. Wanting to be called Miss or Mr. like white folk.

Dear Samuel,

Chicago. Images of Birmingham flood the news. Police turning fire hoses on schoolchildren. Police dogs attacking unarmed schoolchildren kneeling in prayer. Sic em. Sick. Sick. Sick. Where will all this end? Hundreds of children—half-naked, bleeding, herded into pens under the hot sun. Why not herd them into gas chambers and finish the job once and for all? Germany did that only a few years ago. The world stepped back and watched it happen. They gassed children. Nobody seemed to care. That was not the Congo. It happened in a supposedly civilized European nation that produces musicians, poets, artists, philosophers, and scientists. If it could happen there, why not here? Why stop at water hoses? Why stop at police dogs? Just shoot to kill. Lynch them all. Ropes are cheap. Trees are everywhere. Connor is everywhere, directing his police to get them niggers. Someone managed to pick off Shuttlesworth with a high-powered hose and got him hospitalized for a day or two. Not long enough.

Interesting item. Africans at the UN demand intervention. If the UN can get involved with promoting peace in the Congo, why not in Alabama? Boy, does that look bad in the world press. The Feds have to do something at long last. The Klan is busy with its firebombs. So Federal troops come to Alabama to restore order. Token gestures of reconciliation by the white power structure. At the same time the Board of Education expels more than a thousand students for cutting school and taking part in the demonstration. Finally the Alabama Supreme Court validates Boutwell's election as Mayor. So Connor is history. Finally. Three weeks too late. Too late. Too late.

OK, they got the children released on bail. What will the next catastrophe be? I can't imagine that the carnage is over.

I am making money hand over fist here. Making . . . money. Making . . . merry. Making . . . other people merry. Hey, did you hear about what's happening in Birmingham?

Birmingham, England?

No, Birmingham, Alabama. You from around those parts?

No. No.

I mean . . . your accent.

To the people of Chicago, all Southern accents sound the same.

Not from Birmingham, then?

No. No. No.

Me thinks that you doth protest too much.

I will never be from Birmingham. No. Never. Why don't you stop watching the news and try out this new toy that came in from Copenhagen?

Copenhagen, you say?

Yes.

You want to show me how to use it?

You want me to give you a demonstration?

Yes. A demonstration.

Demonstrations are . . . good. I give good demonstrations.

These toys look a little risqué. You're sure we're not breaking any laws?

You're afraid of getting arrested in the privacy of your own home?

Demonstrations can lead to arrests. Do you know the laws of our state?

Laws against demonstrations?

To protect the moral fiber of the populace.

We wouldn't want to disturb the moral character of the populace. Then again, I am trying to preserve the emotional well-being of the populace.

My emotional well-being?

Yours and the enlightened few who respond to demonstrations of this kind.

I think I am responding to your demonstration.

You are responding quite well.

Then you would judge the demonstration to be a success.

There are other demonstrations that can follow.

Good. I can't get enough of your . . . demonstrations. Oh, tell me about Birmingham.

All I know is what I read in the papers.

On TV?
I don't watch TV anymore.
Tell me about your father.
He doesn't write.
Tell me about your mother.
My mother is dead.
Oh.
I killed her.
Oh. Tell me about your children.
No children.
Tell me about your wife.
No wife.
Your family.
No family.
Oh.
I am alone.
Oh.
Without a place to call home.
Oh.
Let me show you . . . more demonstrations.

There were demonstrations in Birmingham. They showed pictures on TV.

I don't watch TV. I told you. No TV.

The children. The hoses. The dogs. The mass arrests.

I don't know. I don't know anything at all.

JUNE 4, 1963

Dear Samuel,

I am back in NYC. Stamp. Food for Peace. Freedom from Hunger. So . . . hungry. I can't seem . . . to get enough to eat. Never enough to eat.

Schools expel students.

Federal Court overturns the expulsions. Orders re-instatement.

Seesaw. Marjorie Daw. Jack shall have a new master.

The Alabama Supreme Court recognizes the new Birmingham government. Jack shall have a new master. Jack can't work any faster. Connor gone. The bastard. The Bull is gone. Gone. Gone. Gone. Gone. Gone. Time to eat. Faster. Faster. Faster. Connor is gone. The bastard. Wrap him round with mustard plaster. From his head to his keister.

JUNE 20, 1963

Dear Samuel,

I missed the UN Airmail Stamp. You can get it from a dealer. Or not. I'm in Wheeling. For the first time. Mountainous. Poor. Mining. Coal. Anthracite. Hill people. Hundredth anniversary of statehood. I think the state was created out to balance Virginia. One free state to balance one slave state. I think West Virginia got the short end of the stick. Not much money to spend on things like carpets. Not much energy or imagination to go beyond the basics in the bedroom. The basics.

Sit-ins in Jackson, Miss. More attack dogs. More arrests. One Civil Rights worker killed. They arrested someone. Probably guilty. No jury will convict him. Not in Mississippi. The Governor stands in the schoolhouse doors to bar admission of Blacks. Backs down in the face of Federal Marshalls. SNCC workers beaten in Winona, Miss., then jailed by police. The President makes a speech on Civil Rights for Negroes. It's all basic, don't you see? Bread and butter. Which side is your bread buttered on? If you let the bread fall, you will discover that you have always buttered it on the wrong side. I'm always on the wrong side. On the outside. Wheeling here and there. Wheeling. Dealing. Far from the center of things. Far, far away.

JULY 1, 1963

Dear Samuel,

Gettysburg. What can I say? The battle took place 100 years ago. It was bloody. Decisive. The stamp, the envelope remembers soldiers on both sides. Pictures both Lincoln and Jefferson Davis. I guess that's only fair. Both decent men, though you won't get many from the South to say so. But a hundred years later, the Post Office is at least willing to acknowledge Davis, not to demonize him. That basic sense of decency seems to be lost these days. Blacks are portrayed as little better than savages, lusting after white women. People march around in sheets, perpetrating atrocities. The new Mayor of Birmingham delays implementation of agreed-upon concessions—and justifies police action as justified homicide. We are getting nowhere fast. Maybe if we had leaders like Lincoln and Davis around—real statesmen. Pipe dreams. Maybe that's the answer. Pipe dreams. A life of wish-fulfillment and fantasy. Right here on the battlefield. I was tempted. I really was. A beautiful girl wandering around. Deeply moved. One step from deeply moved to deeply aroused. A young couple. Possible threesome. Right there in the open field where so many died—needlessly. What better way to commemorate them. It's about time. My whole existence based on the taking of another's life. I should get life without pardon. One way or the other. Let them be horrified at an act of sacrilege. As if what was happening back home was any less a sacrilege. Shooting Medgar Evers in the back. Laughing through the trial knowing nothing would come of it. Sacrilege. One sacrilege leads to another. Am I going to commit the act on the site where a Union soldier died—or a Confederate. Does it matter? Does anything ultimately matter? And if not, anything is permissible. Not only permissible. Desirable. A state of principle—that there are not principles. Anything goes. I am going away from Gettysburg. Getting away. Gettysburg is getting to me. Getting to me. Getting. Gettysburg.

July 12, 1963

Dear Samuel,

Boston. American Air Mail Society Convention, whatever that means. I don't really care. You want the postcard. It's yours. I don't care. Don't seem to care about much these days. Blacks registering en masse in Mississippi. En masse. In Miss-issippi. Another reconstruction. Stimulated by activists from the North again. Carpetbaggers. Stimulated. Aroused. Maybe that's the ticket. Get everyone stimulated. Aroused. Even in Boston. Prim and proper Boston. Can get them aroused about Mississippi and Alabama. Maybe even aroused in Boston. My mission, Get everyone aroused. On Romanian carpets. My purpose in life.

AUGUST 1, 1963

Dear Samuel,

Dayton, Ohio. What could possibly happen in Dayton? A revolution in postal service. Stamps are now overprinted by a luminescent material to speed handling by machines rather than people. I can see some people snicker. The mail is no longer processed by human hands—that is to say, it is processed by Blacks, so for all intents and purposes, not quite human hands. Historical precedent. Maybe just 3/5 human. Still, attitudes can change. Improvement. Now maybe 4/5 human. Enough to let Blacks and Whites meet together to work things out in Birmingham, no less—153 of them. If you integrate the restaurants, do you let these people eat for 4/5 of the regular price? Hardly likely. You want integration—it has its price. Equality. Equality of cost in restaurants. Fair is fair. Did I hear right? Did Birmingham really repeal its segregation ordinances? Whatever happened to Segregation now, Segregation tomorrow, Segregation forever? Forever doesn't last very long these days. I suppose I should be grateful for small blessings. Grateful for something. Grateful that this letter will get to you more efficiently. Did you notice any difference in efficiency? Did you notice the luminescence? How are things in my hometown? Tell me so that if I do come home, it will not take me too long to readjust.

August 17, 1963

Dear Samuel,

DC. Stamp commemorating the second anniversary of the Alliance for Progress. Why honor something that is only two years old? Why not wait a bit and see if it is really initiating progress? That would be progress—and therefore would be blocked in committee.

What is the Alliance for Progress anyway? Who cares? There is a stamp. The envelope has the magic words—First Day of Issue—on it. So it is a collector's item. Who cares what it commemorates? The Third Annual Shit-stomping Festival. The fifth annual cow patty throwing contest. The Betty Crocker animal dung recipe contest. Eat shit, everyone. It's low in fat. It's nutritious. Eat shit. It's the thing to do.

AUGUST 30, 1963

Dear Samuel,

NYC. Postcard with words in French and English. I suppose the French is a translation of the English or vice versa. I wouldn't know. I never took French in school. I suppose I could find someone who could translate for me—even pay someone to do it. That's what the world is coming to. You can't get something for nothing. Not anymore. People don't do anything out of the goodness of their hearts. I am in NYC. I suppose I should have gone to DC. Thousands gathered there. The highlight—Martin Luther King's "I Have A Dream" speech. It's been only two days, and I've seen it on TV countless times. The man certainly knows how to speak. The tradition of Black Baptist preachers working the congregation up until some fall out—inspired by the Holy Spirit. Maybe speaking in tongues. Maybe curing the cripples, the deaf, and the blind. All a question of faith. If you will it, it is no dream. I heard that somewhere or other. A few hundred thousand people with faith. Nothing happens if you believe everything is fine just the way it is. There has to be some discontent. Some discomfort. Some dissatisfaction. Most of those in attendance were Black. Which is OK. You have to start with your own. With action, not words. Words can inspire action, but talk is cheap. These folks are laying their lives on the line to get things moving. Hell, there was even a Rabbi there hobnobbing with King. And that's fine. It's important to know you're not alone. That you have support, direction even from people who don't necessarily agree with every step you're taking. That's the key. They will figure out what they want. If it agrees with what liberals think, that's fine. If it doesn't, even if it fails, it is still helping to define a future. And for better or worse, it's their future they need to define.

I, too, have a dream. I have hesitated to tell it to anyone lest they try to interpret it and I wind up with in interpretation and not the dream itself. Three times removed from reality. Can one ever recapture the exact scene that occurred in the dream? Or its significance? I spoke with a child the other day. His dream was for universal peace. A nice dream. Not going to happen anytime soon. Was it even her dream or maybe her parents' dream they imposed on her.

Like me. Imposing all that racial stuff I knew empirically was a bunch of shit. But what did it leave me? Once the dream they foisted on me proved to be false, what was I left with? Nothing much at all. I don't have those kinds of dreams anymore. Just provisional, expedited dreams that people will stop killing each other. Maybe the dreams are catching. Catching. Like King's. A real rouser. I imagined I was in a church. Quite a church. Al fresco. Any preacher would give his eyeteeth to be able to speak at a church like that before a crowd like that. As it happens, I am beginning to have problems with my teeth. I've lost a few. Chewing is tricky sometimes. Not terribly aesthetic to go around with strategic teeth missing. I feel like a red-neck or even worse. People judge you by your appearance. It's hard to convince them that you're intelligent, that they should trust your judgment, when you look like a yokel. I may have to get some dental work done. The only thing is I don't stay in any one place very long, and generally I don't have much money for that kind of thing. So I guess I'll have to keep looking like a hick and hope people will get past their first impression and find out that I'm a good businessman. Honest but persuasive. If you can't sell a refrigerator to an Eskimo on an ice floe, you shouldn't go into sales in the first place. I've gotten to the point where I can sell a refrigerator to an Eskimo. I'm not sure I could sell Civil Rights to my father and his friends. I've given up on that one. I'll have to be satisfied with carpets and dildos.

OCTOBER 1, 1963

Dear Samuel,

NYC. Things getting weirder and weirder. A stamp to commemorate the West New Guinea Operation—the transfer of ownership, as it were, to Indonesia. What is that about? I can't begin to understand. I don't care to understand. There are things happening in the world I don't want to have to think about. At the end of Candide, after all the atrocities the characters have witnessed and experienced, they all withdraw into a small corner of the world to tend a garden. Let the world go on its merry way. Its not-so-merry way. But where is my garden? Not in New Guinea. Funny. In the middle of Manhattan, amidst all the skyscrapers and tenement houses, you can find small gardens. Absolutely amazing. And there is Central Park. One can get lost in Central Park. There are places in this city where you can be alone—or nearly alone. Sometimes I come across a couple of lovers under a bush or a tree—or a poetic soul or a painter, sometimes someone drunk or in a drug stupor. One could wander through Central Park for weeks and not know that the rest of the world exists. Like West New Guinea. Indonesia. Birmingham. One of the newspapers here called it Bombingham. After the 16th Street Baptist church was bombed. And the four girls were killed. The four girls. Four girls. Four more. Tell me how people are dealing with this. Tell me. I need to know.

The Governor uses troopers to block integration around the state. Did he lower the flags in the Capitol half-mast? The President sends National Guardsmen to help integrate the schools in Birmingham. The Black students are greeted with jeers and curses. Such hatred and abuse directed at schoolchildren. I saw pictures of them in a newspaper covering the face of some homeless man sleeping on a bench in the park. Pictures of the children. Pictures of the white parents and children jeering at them. Which is the greatest atrocity? Though I walk through the valley of the shadow of death, I will fear no evil. Do the children fear no evil? Their parents? The parents of the four that died. The jeerers. The bomber. Fear no evil. The evil is there. The fears.

The all-white delegation to the National Democratic Convention walked out of the Convention. They refused to sign on to the Party Platform affirming Civil Rights. They secede. It is the Civil War all over again—or as the homeboys would put it, the War of Northern Aggression. Tell that to the parents of the four that died. Tell them about Northern Aggression. The others whose homes have been bombed. The ones that have been shot or lynched. The local police arrest no one. If it ever does come to trial, no one will be convicted. Only the Federal government will investigate. The Federal judges who block the use of state troopers sent out by the Governor to block integration. We are at war again. And somehow, it seems significant to someone to commemorate the transfer of power in West New Guinea. I am writing to you from a bench in Central Park. There is a couple not far away making love behind a bush. I hear their moans. The sounds of ecstasy. They don't need my toys. My toys. Locked up in my van for a month now. I am running out of money. I will have to get back to what I do soon. To make ends meet. Some more demonstrations. All I really want to do is tend my garden and let the world go on its merry way.

October 5, 1963

Dear Samuel,

The stamp honors Cordell Hull—American statesman. Senator from Tennessee. Secretary of State under President Roosevelt from 1933–1944. Winner of the Nobel Peace Prize in 1946. I'm not sure what he did to deserve the award. It must have been something noteworthy. Maybe it would be nice to have him go down to Birmingham to work things out—that is, if he is still alive. An elder statesman. Transfer sovereignty to Indonesia. Might be a big improvement. Saw two muggings last night in Central Park. Could do nothing but watch. Here in my garden. They are forcing me to leave my garden. Forcing me. To leave. My garden.

October 14, 1963

Dear Samuel,

DC again. The stamp honors the Tenth Anniversary of the National Academy of Science. Sounds like a noteworthy institution. Every country needs an Academy of Science. I wonder what it's been doing of late. The application of biological principles to study the interaction of subspecies in an urban environment. Black and White in Birmingham. Maybe someone could make sense of that. I read a study once about rat populations. Urban rat populations. One group will recognize a member of another group that enters its territory. Did I tell you about that already? I forget.

The Bible says to welcome the stranger that is in your midst, for you were strangers in the land of Egypt. You were slaves. You know the heart of a slave. A former slave. The grandchild of a slave. Don't people read the Bible anymore? Everybody goes to church. Don't the Ministers read the Bible? Be like rats. Keep the strangers out. If they invade, kill them. Kill them all. Eat their flesh. Here are four new recipes. For the tender flesh of four new victims of bombings. Half-roasted already. I, Gulliver, don't want to be identified with such Yahoos. Find me some noble horses I can associate with. Find me some hay I can munch on. The smell of half-roasted flesh is noxious to my brain. My stomach churns. Find me some hay before I gag.

October 26, 1963

Dear Samuel,

I'm still in DC. They are celebrating the first luminescent commemorative stamp. It glows green under special lights. Commemorating the hundredth anniversary of City Mail Delivery. I suppose that is something to commemorate. I manage somehow to keep in touch—at least with you. The Mayor is still ignoring recommendation of a bi-racial committee to deal with the situation in Birmingham. The Mayor who was supposed to be a political moderate. Certainly better than Bull Connor would have been. But obviously not much better. Maybe he doesn't perpetrate or incite atrocities. He just doesn't do much to prevent them.

Do not stand by idly and watch as your brother's blood is shed. That's from the Bible. Why am I quoting the Bible so much of late? Maybe I should have become a preacher and give sermons on the passages people don't want to read or understand. I don't think I would last very long. Just talk to us about religious matters—Heaven and Hell and Salvation. I don't think people would want to hear me talk about that either. I am more like a prophet in the wilderness, shouting my message to the empty air. Except that I have no prophetic message to bring even to the empty air. No message. No vision. I just wander around, selling my toys as Rome burns—and people squeeze out one more orgiastic night before destruction is complete.

October 29, 1963

Dear Samuel,

A stamp to honor the hundredth anniversary of the International Red Cross and founder, Henri Durant. From the spelling of his name, apparently a Frenchman. OK, Monsieur Durant. Where is the International Red Cross when we need it? Where were you after the church was bombed? When the children got hit with the water hoses? When the dogs slashed their flesh? Or do you only send your workers to West New Guinea and the Congo?

NOVEMBER 1, 1963

Dear Samuel,

November 1—traditionally the date the Post Office issues its Christmas stamps. I traveled to Santa Claus, Indiana. Yes, there is such a place. On state highway 162 about forty miles east of Evansville. Look, it could be worse. A town has to pick a name for itself. Somewhere in Southern Alabama, they could decide to name a town Connorsville or Bull City or Wallaceburg. Don't kid yourself. A town can name itself after Jolly Saint Nicholas and still behave badly. Southern Indiana is more like the Deep South than like the North. I passed a billboard that purportedly showed Martin Luther King at a Communist training camp. And remember the Klan was active here in the '20s. So . . . Santa Claus, Indiana. Ho. Ho. Ho. Only fifty or so days before Christmas. I'm dreaming of a White Christmas just like the ones I used to know. May your dreams be merry and bright. And may all your Christmases be White. And whoever heard of black snow? Really. Or white snow streaked with black? It just ain't natural. Nothing much to do in Santa Claus, Indiana. I'll be headed back East again.

NOVEMBER 4, 1963

Dear Samuel,

The tenth anniversary of the UN facility in NYC. Maybe it was a mistake to move it here from Geneva. I'm not sure the Swiss are any better than we are. They handle their social problems by not granting foreigners citizenship however long they stay. They import foreign laborers for a time. They're not allowed to stay permanently. That's one way of handling the problem. They declare this neutrality. In the face of Nazi atrocities all over Europe, they maintained their neutrality. How can one remain neutral in the face of atrocity? I suppose you could say that enabled them to avoid an invasion by the German army. Then again, their banks profited by safeguarding Nazi money. And they weren't big on accepting refugees from Nazi persecution. So maybe Geneva was not such a good place after all. And if not New York, then where? If you dig beneath the surface, every nation has a past it shouldn't be proud of. Our problems may be more glaring than others, but others are no better. Sometimes worse, as hard as that might be to imagine.

I hear that they have started hiring black officers on the police force in scattered cities around Alabama. Is that really true? Are they allowed to carry guns? What would happen if they tried to arrest a white person for speeding or drunk driving? Give a Klansman a ticket for reckless driving in a school zone or alleged possession of firearms and explosives. What oh what is the world coming to? What happens if they tried to arrest my father? I could see his mouth open in amazement as he got handcuffed and put in the backseat of the patrol car. "I am being arrested by a frigging black nigger cop. What is this world coming to when a Whiteman can't weave his car through traffic without a nigger cop arresting him." What indeed.

December 7, 1963

Dear Samuel,

Henderson, Kentucky. A beautiful stamp honoring John J. Audubon. I have been traveling through small towns here and there just listening to people talk about the assassination of President Kennedy. Conspiracy theories. Expressions of grief and despair. Anguish and confusion. Or just resignation. I don't want to go too far South. I can imagine that many people are happy to see him gone. A Yankee imposing integration on the South with Federal troops. But Eisenhower did it before him. And the new President—Lyndon Johnson—from Texas, no less, has sworn to carry out Kennedy's legislative initiative, including those concerning Civil Rights. And the word is that come what may, Johnson will push, shove, or ram that legislation through. There is nothing subtle about that man, and he knows how to get things done. The Southerners who were glad to get rid of Kennedy will get nostalgic about him once they meet a fellow redneck who can out-cuss them and beat them at their own game. Image of a grieving wife and grieving children. Of people in tears as the casket heads for final burial—the victims of shootings and bombings and lynchings. I am heading back to NYC. The year is coming to an end. I don't know if there is anything to look forward to. Central Park will be stark and bare for the winter—cold and grey. I feel cold and grey. Funny how we look for a place and time to reflect on feelings. A rainy night in Georgia. I feel like it is raining all over the world.

DECEMBER 18, 1963

Dear Samuel,

NYC. The United Nations. The 15th anniversary of the Universal Declaration of Human Rights. Sure. Tell that to the families of the four girls that died in the 16th Street Baptist Church. Go tell it on the mountain. Over the hills and everywhere. Go tell it on the mountain. And in Central Park. I'll be there. Tending my garden.

January 10, 1964

Dear Samuel,

Houston, Texas. Yes. Texas. Deep South. Sort of. Lyndon B. Johnson territory. I wanted to see how Texans are responding to having one of their own running the country. Most Texans come across as being politically conservative. Johnson is going to be unabashedly liberal in his agenda. Nothing subtle about the man. A hundred years ago he would be packing two six-shooters, and if you didn't like what he said, he would meet you on the street in front of the saloon and shoot it out with you. This is still frontier country. Big. Brash. Oil country. A lot of money to flash around. We grabbed the land from Mexico. Nothing pretty about that. Manifest Destiny. Indians on the land we wanted? Get rid of them one way or another. Mexicans? Start a war. Win the war. The stamp honors Sam Houston—Texas soldier and statesman. First President of the Texas Republic. And when Texas became a state, he became one of its Senators. Of a slave state. Some stories about that. Some escaping slaves thought that Texas was a free state. They made it to the Sabine River, discovered their mistake, and took their chances on the Louisiana side, setting up all-black towns. Discretion is the better part of valor. Don't mess with Texas. Don't mess with Texans. Thoreau wouldn't pay his taxes, because he didn't approve of how the U.S. government was provoking wars to grab land from Mexico. They put him in jail. He wrote Civil Disobedience. I don't think they beat him up or put him on a chain gang the way they might have done in Texas. Someone paid his taxes, so after a day he was free to go back to Walden Pond. He didn't protest too much at that point. He had made his point. Sharp point. Like a barb. Pointed straight at the nation's heart. Big deal. Slavery didn't end. The landgrab in the Southwest didn't end. The distortion of history. Remember the Alamo. Santa Ana as the big villain. History belongs to the winners. We condemned Hitler for the landgrab in Danzig and Sudatenland. Rightly so. Germany lost the war. Had to give anything back. I don't notice too many people in

Houston ready and willing to become part of Mexico again. Or ready and willing to give any land back to the Indians.

Or in Birmingham. The Mayor's Committee on Human Relations recommends the hiring of Black cops and firemen, reducing discrimination in schools, hiring and upgrading Black municipal workers. The Mayor rejects this recommendation and accuses the Committee of overstepping its advisory role. The Bull is gone. Long live Mayor Boutwell. Not quite a bull. A cow in bull's clothing. I've had enough of Texas. I'm heading North again.

January 13, 1964

Dear Samuel,

NYC. The UN. Inter-Governmental Maritime Consultative Organization, whatever that means. Possibly that different nations can agree that they have a common interest in certain policies with regard to the oceans. Can overcome narrow nationalistic interests to work for the common good of humanity. A nice goal. But the Organization has no teeth. No enforcement powers. No better than the Mayor's Committee in Birmingham. The Mayor can set the Committee up, let them talk, come to a consensus, and then he can ignore their recommendations. So what good is talk? There has to be a way of moving from talk to action. There I go, sounding like some kind of radical. My talk. No action. I should be on the front lines somewhere demanding change. Instead I'm back in Central Park jammering away. I hear that seven Blacks passed the written text to join the police force in Birmingham. You think that will impress the Mayor? What will it take to impress the Mayor? More Federal troops? Maybe the Mayor will be in a car accident and a black cop will save his life. Like the old story of the Black football player that raced for the winning touchdown in a game. Look at that Injun run. Look at that Injun run.

April 22, 1964

Dear Samuel,

It has been a while since I have written. Three months. Where has the time gone? I met a woman—of course. That explains everything. Maybe not quite everything. A New York sophisticate. And that is saying something, since most New Yorkers see themselves as being highly sophisticated. Sophistication is imbibed in their mother's milk. Except, of course, that most New Yorkers are too sophisticated to nurse their babies. Maybe some do. Maybe it's more sophisticated now to glorify the natural and it's the common people who think they're imitating the upper classes by using formula. Are you thoroughly confused now?

The woman was certainly not going back to Nature. She showed me poems by the French writer Baudelaire. He celebrated city life. Ultra, ultra refinement, which often wound up being ultra perverse. None of this nonsense of justifying perversion as being natural. The triumph of man is the celebration of the synthetic—the artificial. Culture is the imposition of mind on Nature. Man is by definition unnatural. You could say it's in his very nature to be so. And if so, why not take artificiality to an extreme? Operate as much as possible in the realm of intellect, not impulse. And what better arena to demonstrate the triumph of the mind over the body than in sexuality—which is supposed to be one of the strongest impulses.

It turned out that the lady—I was going to say, the woman, but that has a more natural connotation—this sophisticated lady had already used just about all the toys I had to offer. For her they were just kindergarten toys she had outgrown long ago. She showed me paraphernalia I never knew existed. That I never would have imagined existed. I quickly went from demonstration and teacher to pupil. I won't even begin to tell you what I learned from her. It wasn't exclusively S and M, but that was a major focus. We went both ways. Here it was not like playing the role of perpetrator and victim but investigating the limits—the possibilities of human responsiveness.

She insisted on this. We were to be equals. Neither submissive nor controlling. Just two adventurers.

I will admit to you that I got a bit lost in the process. I started out at this game just to earn a living—to enable me to move freely across the landscape. OK, there were some pleasant escapades along the way. But this was like a graduate course in self-awareness and self-discovery. I could write a book on what I learned. I'm not sure anyone would be willing to publish it. The censor would have a field day cutting and slicing. I barely read the papers. I barely watched the news on TV. I was in a zone where time ceased to exist. Where Birmingham ceased to exist. I don't know how long I could have stayed in this no-man's land, but one day she woke up, looked at me, and said it's over. I could leave now.

Just like that. I could face the world again. The everyday world. That was enough. I went to the library. I checked some news magazines to find out what I had missed. You could have told me the whole world had disappeared, and I would have taken it in stride.

But the world was still there. A little different from before. The 24th Amendment abolished the poll tax for Federal elections. Only for Federal elections. But the impact would be felt—a substantial increase in the number of Black voters in the Deep South. A few more Civil Rights workers killed in Selma. Malcolm X assassinated in NYC. I was right here, and I didn't know. Killed by Blacks unhappy with his defection from the Black Muslims. That was an interesting development. I had been reading up on that group. I told you that. They don't want integration because they think Whites are an inferior race. That's a twist. They take a militant stand on White aggression but basically just want to be left alone. I'm not sure why Malcolm X wanted to leave the fold. Strange that they would show more aggression against one of their number than to their stereotypic enemy, but I guess each group gets sensitive when it comes to those they think of as traitors to the cause. I don't think I would be too popular in certain circles back home.

So what's going on? The World's Fair in NY. Fun and games. The world came to NY to show off its culture, its science and industry. You think there might be a time the world would come to a place like Atlanta or Houston? Not yet. I am eating all kinds of exotic foreign food and am enjoying it immensely. I like to eat. My mentor for the past few months would have pointed to the food and talked about culture vs. nature. Man will eat almost anything, but he will usually doctor it up one way or another and call it cuisine rather than food. I am stuffing myself full of cuisine. I am a cultural creature. Animals graze and eat whatever they can find. I dine. And drink. And dine. What can I tell you? I have a healthy appetite. I will have to go on a major diet. I will begin to look like a cultural blimp.

April 29, 1964

Dear Samuel,

Cross country in six days. Martinez, California—to commemorate John Muir, a conservationist before there were even terms for such people. He was the one who almost single-handedly saved the remaining redwood forests. Gave birth to the Sierra Club. See, one person can make a difference. Or not. I can be inspired by such folk, but inspired to do what? Inspired by those who put their lives on the line to help Blacks register to vote—to integrate libraries and playgrounds. Inspired . . . to do . . . what?

MAY 5, 1964

Dear Samuel,

I didn't make it back to NY for a regular airmail stamp. You can get that from a dealer. I headed back for Fredericksburg, Virginia. One hundredth anniversary of the Battle of the Wilderness. I don't know much about that battle, but the envelope has pictures of Grant and Lee on it. After a hundred years, I suppose one can acknowledge the generals of both the winning and the losing sides. Will it take a hundred years before we can do that for the current battle? Martin Luther King and the Reverend Shuttlesworth on one side, the Mayor and Bull Connor on the other—or maybe Governor Wallace. Somehow I don't think so. General Lee was a gentleman who fought for what he believed in. Somehow I can't give Wallace that much credit. Maybe in 500 years we'll be able to put all this in perspective—put the dogs and the fire hoses behind us. The burning crosses and the lynchings, the way we put the auto de fes and the witch trials behind us, torturing people to get them to confess to whatever. I get a tour of the battleground. It's peaceful now. How many paid for that peace with their lives? For what? Perhaps there's a just war, and it makes sense to ask people to sacrifice for an ideal—for survival of the nation, for preserving a way of life. Most people stumble into wars that have little rhyme or reason. The two opposing sides here chatted with each other at night and shot at each other in the morning. Make sense of that. It's like playing chess with someone, but at the end of the game someone gets shot. Maybe both get shot. The stamp almost induces a feeling of nostalgia. A nostalgia for amputated limbs and gangrene. For widows and orphans. There was a book written about apartheid in South Africa a few years ago. *Cry, the Beloved Country.* That's it, exactly. *Cry, the Beloved Country.* I stood in the battlefield, and I wept uncontrollably. I didn't know I had that many tears to shed. And then . . . I fled.

MAY 9, 1964

Dear Samuel,

NYC. It almost feels like home. A UN stamp honoring the Secretaries General—Dag Hammerskjold, U Thant, Trygve Lee. Lyndon Johnson is to address the General Assembly. I'm not sure what he will be speaking about. Possibly the war in Viet Nam. Asking young men to sacrifice—for what? I'm sure he'll come up with something. They always do.

June 15, 1964

Dear Samuel,

Another month gone by. I've been remiss. Wandering around NYC as if there were some purpose in it. OK. Today I have purpose. The UN stamp honors a Conference on Trade and Development held in Geneva. If I hurry I can make it down to Elizabeth, New Jersey, to commemorate the 300th anniversary of statehood. Elizabeth is not too far from NYC. I should be able to make it there and back without too much trouble—so that I can continue my wanderings. Find a place to eat. Maybe take in a movie. Not much news coverage these days from Birmingham—from the Deep South in general. Are things quieting down finally? Are people coming to their senses? Or is the Northern press just getting bored with the whole business?

July 22, 1964

Dear Samuel,

I can't take the streets of NYC anymore. Time for another trip. Out West. Selling stuff wherever I go. I guess this justifies my traveling. Some beautiful country out there. I've been to a few more National Parks. Hiking. That's reason enough. The Nevada Centennial is in Carson City. They had a mint here once. That made sense. If you dig up the silver locally, why ship it somewhere else to be minted? I had a silver dollar from Carson City once. You could tell. It had a *CC* on it. Coins minted in San Francisco had an *S*. New Orleans had an *O*. Denver had a *D*. Philadelphia either a *P* or nothing. I don't think they mint coins in New Orleans or Carson City anymore. I don't know about San Francisco. I don't think they'll be minting silver coins anymore. I'm not sure why that disturbs me. A quarter will still be a quarter. Some changes bother me. Some status quo bothers me. Some contradiction here. Maybe it's a Southern thing. Like Faulkner bemoaning the loss of Southern tradition—the elegance, the gentility—even while he acknowledged the price paid by Blacks to maintain it. The tragic sense of life. You can't win for losing.

AUGUST 1, 1964

Dear Samuel,

Washington DC. The stamp says Register to Vote. That's what they're trying to do in Alabama, Mississippi, and Louisiana. The President says, "For our Democracy to flourish, it is vital for every eligible American to register to vote." I guess the key word here is eligible. And the criteria for eligibility seem to be determined by the white power structure. I heard a joke the other day. The gist is that Irish, Italian, and White Anglo-Saxon Protestants have to spell "God" and name the first President of the United States. Blacks have to spell "Chrysanthemum' and name the deputy sheriff of Toomsuba County. Did I tell you that before? My memory is not too clear these days. A bit out of touch. Let's see.

Blacks in Mississippi create the Freedom Democratic Party, because the regular party won't send any Blacks as delegates to the National Convention. Now it's a question of who the national party will seat at the Convention.

Three Civil Rights workers killed—Philadelphia, Miss. Black and white equality at last. Two whites and one black murdered. All buried in the same levee. In Philadelphia, city of brotherly love. Maybe in Mississippi they don't know what the name of their town actually means. Either that or they don't care.

And . . . July 2. How could I have missed the signing of the Civil Rights Act. I'm not sure what that will mean. There are a lot of Southern Democrats who aren't going to be terribly happy about that. It suspends literacy tests and knowledge or character tests in areas where fewer than 50% of the people are registered to vote. The Attorney General justified the passage as a Federal law under the Interstate Commerce clause of the Constitution. I'm not sure how that works. They'll probably test the new law in the Supreme Court.

So . . . a wave of new Black voters. It should make a difference in areas where there is a Black majority in the population. For some whites it will feel like Reconstruction all over again.

AUGUST 14, 1964

Dear Samuel,

I'm up in Stratford, Conn., to celebrate the 400th anniversary of Shakespeare's birth. It's an attractive stamp really, with an Elizabethan feel to the design. Words taken from Hamlet, Act IV, Scene I. I'd rather have the quote, "Something is rotten in the state of Denmark." A law passed in Congress guarantees Federal funds for Native Americans for legal counsel in civil and criminal suits—legal counsel from the American Bar Association. In all the hurly burly of the struggle for Civil Rights for Blacks, Native Americans have been largely overlooked. Maybe they'll learn some tactics that have been used successfully by Blacks. Traditionally Indians have been less accommodating to white cultures and white rule. The result has been confrontation—and you know who came out on top. The Indians signed treaties. The treaties were broken. Another confrontation. Another massacre. The Trail of Tears. Forced migration to a stretch of barren land where they could either freeze to death or starve. Strange to have a bill like this passed at this time. You'd think all the attention would be somewhere else.

The Voting Rights bill is signed. The Mississippi Freedom Democratic Party is challenging the seating of the all-white delegation at the National Convention. It will be interesting to see how they work this out. How Lyndon Johnson will work it out.

September 11, 1964

Dear Samuel,

Time is passing. I'm on the road again. Rochester, Minnesota. A stamp to honor the two brothers who founded the Mayo Clinic. The quote—not terribly inspiring—goes, "They revered the truth and sought to know." The clinic is well-known. Probably deserving of recognition. It's already cold in Minnesota. People joke about that around here. Minnesota has two seasons—July/August and winter. I don't think I'm prepared for weather like this. Then again, I'm receiving a lot of home hospitality. Whether it's due to Midwest friendliness or compassion for a poor Southerner that can't take the cold. They tell me that there are weeks on end that the temperature never gets above zero. Hopefully I'll be gone by then. I sold some carpets. A whole lot of toys. I guess people get bored up here in winter. They have to do something to keep themselves occupied. OK, most of them have been raised in pretty straightlaced Protestant homes—mainly Lutheran. I don't know how Lutherans regard the kind of amusements I'm selling. Whatever they preach, sales are going well. Maybe they do stuff just so they can feel guilty about it afterwards. I don't really care. They can buy the toys for pleasure or to stimulate guilt. I've given a few demonstrations along the way. Not a bad job being a teacher. Nice side benefits. I'm heading back to NYC to restock.

September 21, 1964

Dear Samuel,

UN issue—at least two stamps on controlling narcotics traffic. Image of a Chinese-looking opium user. He doesn't look too happy or too healthy. Stamps with drug paraphernalia. Couldn't it pique someone's curiosity to do a little experimentation with such exotic equipment? The suggestion is that the Chinese are the ones addicted to heroin. But I've encountered a lot of addicts around the U.S., and not one was Chinese. I met a woman in upstate New York. Small town. Her kids were going to a Catholic school—seventh and ninth grades. The woman got a notice from the principal's office to be aware of the rampant use of heroin among the students—that and the prevalence of syphilis and unwanted pregnancies. Small town, USA. It used to be fashionable to use drugs. Quincey—*Confession of an English Opium Eater*. Coleridge writing "Kubla Khan" under the influence. It used to be legal. People used laudanum for colds. Coca-Cola used to have a bit of cocaine in it. The world didn't fall apart. There are any number of people I'd like to get hooked on something or other. Keep them so preoccupied with hallucinations, they wouldn't have time for anything else. Maybe get them hooked on sex toys as well. So preoccupied, that if someone came and told them it was time for a cross burning or a church bombing, they'd wave it off. Later, man, I'm too busy tripping out. Later, man, me and my wife are into it. But they're integrating the schools. You know, I don't really care anymore. Why don't you sample some of my stash. A better high than you'd get at a lynching—that may be the answer to the whole problem. Get everybody high. Then it doesn't matter who else is in the room. It may not matter who you're doing it with either. One big happy, mellow world.

SEPTEMBER 26, 1964

Dear Samuel,

I'm in DC. The new stamp commemorates Social Security—For the People. By the People. Where have I heard that line before? Oh, yes, the Gettysburg Address. You can't fool me. I'm not quite ready for Social Security yet. I'm not sure I'd qualify anyway. I do a cash business. When I get old and grey, I may not have a safety net. It's OK. I'll just lie out under a tree and wait for death. Maybe I'll jump off a cliff into the sea. In the eyes of the church, I will have committed a mortal sin. If you suffer, it must mean that God wants you to suffer. Just bear your cross. God never gives you more than you can bear. I don't believe that. You get to a stage where there is no quality to your life—just end it, pure and simple. I wouldn't step out in front of a car. That wouldn't be fair to the driver. Besides, it's messy. Someone has to clean up after you and bury you. Better to find some deserted spot, do what you have to do, and let the vultures and the ants take care of the remains. And me, I'm not afraid of eternal punishment in an afterlife. We're here. We live. We die. And that's that. No Final Judgment. Just . . . oblivion. I realize that cuts into some pretty basic religious beliefs, but that's OK. Let people believe what they will. At the end of a long day, I welcome sleep. Death's other kingdom. The next morning, surprise, I wake up. At the end of an exhausting life, I slip into a permanent sleep. No morning. No awakening. So . . . maybe no need for Social Security. Let others use it. It's OK with me. I didn't ask to come into existence. I won't ask anyone for permission to leave. Sorry if this disappoints you. That's just what I believe—or rather don't believe. No telling if any views change tomorrow—or next year. Was it Emerson who wrote that consistency was the hobgoblin of small minds? Emerson was a deep thinker. If he could accept inconsistencies in his own character, who am I to differ with him? I'm heading out West again. New route. New scenery. I think by the time all this is over, I should know the country coast to coast.

October 5, 1964

Dear Samuel,

Roswell, New Mexico. The stamp honors Dr. Robert Goddard—the father of modern rocketry. I seem to recall something else about Roswell. Maybe it will come to me later.

Small tidbit I picked up in a newspaper. The families of some soldiers killed in Viet Nam wanted their loved ones buried in Elmwood Cemetery in Birmingham—with all due honors. They weren't allowed to do that. They die fighting for our country, but that doesn't entitle them to be buried in the same cemetery as white soldiers killed in the same war. Equal opportunity to die but not to be buried wherever. Segregation trumps patriotism. A matter of principle, don't you see.

OCTOBER 15, 1964

Dear Samuel,

Back in NYC. I think now it's less a question of being in one city or another as moving—being on the road. Always on the road to somewhere and then to somewhere else. I'm not sure why. Nothing seems to hold me for very long.

The stamp—Fiftieth Anniversary of the American Society of Composers, Authors and Publishers, ASCAP. A picture of eight White men—in the center is Victor Herbert. Maybe he was the first president. Back in 1914. Wasn't that the Vaudeville era? Most of the song and dance men and the comedians were either Jewish, Irish, or Black. You wouldn't know that from the picture. There's a lot you wouldn't know unless you get past the pictures. All men, by the way. Weren't there any female singers and such? Even female composers. I can't think of any offhand. I remember one female comic—Fanny Brice. She was Jewish. Then there was Burns and Allen. And Lucille Ball. Ethel Merman. I could probably think of more. So . . . the Jews, the Irish, and the Blacks—and the women did the performing, and the white men ran the organization. Why am I not surprised? I'll stick around here for a while. Maybe re-establish contact with that ultra-sophisticated person I wrote to you about. The next commemorative comes out in Honolulu. You'll have to get that one from a dealer. My car can't get me there nohow.

NOVEMBER 9, 1964

Dear Samuel,

I'm in Bethelem, Pa. A good place to issue a Christmas stamp. So many towns in the U.S. named after Biblical places. A lot named after Indians. We killed them, ran the survivors off, and then named towns, counties, and states after them. We use them as mascots for high school teams. Pro teams as well—the Indians, the Braves, the Redskins, and what have you. As if after we massacred them, we could glorify the courage and emulate their virtues and abilities on and off the field. Along with predatory animals we wipe out whenever and wherever we find them.

I saw a picture of the Homemakers stamp. Fiftieth anniversary of Smith-Lever Act, whatever that was. "Home is where the heart is." OK. Picture of a man at home with the kids. Dad is leaving for work, briefcase in hand. An Ozzie and Harriet, Leave it to Beaver, Father Knows Best kind of family. Not too many families like that anymore. Is that a good or a bad thing?

DECEMBER 2, 1964

Dear Samuel,

December. Another year almost gone. By all criteria it has not been a very happy year. I spent a lot of time in the National Gallery of Art. Somehow art is soothing to my soul. I like the Impressionists and how they deal with the beauty of Nature. But it's not only that. I enjoy even the works of Goya. The dark side of human nature. War. Savagery. Painters—artists in general have a choice in life. They can go off to one side and scream and shout—weep, mourn, despair—or they can choose to pick up a brush and paint. And the despair ends. There. You can look at a portrayal of a firing squad—even if you imagine that the victim is innocent or is fighting for a just cause against tyranny, the act of painting it on canvas engages an audience of like-minded people who will respond to the scene in a way that might address the injustice. In the process, the artist has to choose appropriate colors—work out the composition—so that there is an affirmation of the artistic process itself. The victim may be dead. The artist as well. But the picture survives, commemorating the victim and the artist. Art can't help but be an affirmation of life itself. I . . . would give anything to be an artist. A poet. Unfortunately, I was not granted the gift. I've tried. Poetry. I have. It doesn't work for me. I read poetry. Even some not-so-good poetry. My meager efforts by comparison are just that. I might as well enter the Olympics in high-board diving. If I somehow managed to survive the fall—and I never did learn how to swim. The pond near my home was no deeper than my chest. I could splash around and even duck under the water, but I never did learn to swim.

What did I learn to do? Somehow I learned to sell—how to get over on people. To sell them my toys and demonstrate how to use them well. I suppose that's something. Hardly what you would put on a tombstone. I look at the stamp—Stuart Davis, an abstract painting. I didn't know of his work before. I'm not sure why the Post Office chose him among the many other abstract painters of his time. But I envy him—not for the fact that his work is on a stamp, but that he can produce works like that at all. Somehow I feel the need to get back to NYC. I have to find that lady again. The time I was with her, I seemed to have a sense of purpose and direction in my life. If the mystics are right, any human activity can lead to enlightenment. The Kama Sutra purports to be a religious text. Certain forms of Buddhism use sex as a path to enlightenment. The Hindu temples are filled with images of the gods involved with all kinds of sexual activity. Maybe I was a Hindu or a Buddhist in a previous life. More likely I'm just seeking out the one thing, for whatever reason, that can preoccupy me body and soul—at any level at all. Whatever that means. If anything means anything at all. When everything is said and done.

December 7, 1964

Dear Samuel,

NYC again. A UN stamp honors Education for Progress. Reduce illiteracy and promote cultural exchange. Again, the focus is on the Third World out there, not the Third World in the U.S.

I can't seem to make contact with my "friend." A feeling of desperation begins to creep in. What if I never find her? What then? I have begun to focus on children as they pass—young adolescents—to fantasize about them. The usual S and M stuff—both ways. Dominating them and being dominated by them. Something is going on in my brain. I'm not sure what. I'm not sure I want to find out.

Racial demonstrations in Harlem and Philadelphia turn violent. No refuge here. No refuge anywhere at all.

JANUARY 6, 1965

Dear Samuel,

DC. Regular issue stamp—Lincoln, the Liberty Bell, Jackson, an old ship (what is that about?). Martin Luther King is awarded the Nobel Peace Prize—gets the recognition he would never have gotten in his native South. In his hometown even. The Supreme Court upholds the Civil Rights Act of 1964. Nothing new. The Feds say one thing. The South pretends nothing has changed. It's like the meeting of an irresistible force and an unmovable object. Something has to give eventually. I fear the moment when it does. I fear that that moment is approaching fast. That the center will not hold. When crises arise, more often than not the extremes pull everyone to one side or the other. Moderates get labeled traitors by both extremes. Lessons of history. History be damned. We are not puppets. We can make choices. It's a new year. Anything is possible.

Regular Air Mail stamp to be issued in Chicago. Can't get there in time. Stamp to be issued on January 8 to commemorate the 150th anniversary of the Battle of New Orleans—the last battle of the War of 1812. The British marched toward the Americans in linear formation, and the American sharpshooters mowed them down. All this after the war was officially over. So sorry, Mr. Redcoat. You fought for nothing, but you're still dead.

I met someone who fought in Korea. He went to the latrine, and when he came back, everyone else in the trench was dead. They awarded him a medal—for what? For figuring out the right moment to move his bowels. We won the Battle of New Orleans. I don't suppose the British have issued a commemorative for the battle they lost. Someone told me there is a huge hall in Versailles with massive pictures commemorating all the battles the French won throughout their history. Of course, there are no pictures commemorating the battles they lost (they would have to have a hall three times the size or more). In any case, I can't get down to New Orleans in time. I'm not sure I would want to go anyway—although it seems that New Orleans has gotten through the integration process relatively peacefully. Then again, New Orleans is not a typical Southern town. I don't know the history. Might be interesting to look into it. You can get the stamps from the dealer. I'm headed back to NYC to resupply. To try to find that lady. Again. As soon as possible. I've started to get some rather obsessive thoughts. If I have to work out my fantasies, it would be better to work them out with her.

JANUARY 25, 1965

Dear Samuel,

NYC. I still can't find her. I did find someone else though. Different. Earthier. More a woman than a lady. Maybe that's not such a bad thing now. She's . . . intuitive. She lets things happen spontaneously—more from whim than from thought. Almost playful, but at times it seems like a thin crust over a lake of molten lava. I don't know how to explain it. We start off playfully; then for some reason, I really want to hurt her, and then it's not make believe anymore. I don't want to turn her into a victim. I want her to submit willfully because I know she can take anything I throw at her, and she dishes it out to me with gusto when we reverse roles. I'm not sure how much more of this I can handle. One of us is going to wind up seriously hurt or even killed. I'm not ready to exit the scene yet. There are a lot of areas where I want to find out how things turn out.

February 15, 1965

Dear Samuel,

DC. A bit worse for wear. But the wounds aren't noticeable. Ironically, the new stamp is about physical fitness—the image of a nude male, ostensibly a Greek statue of a discus thrower. The dedication is to Dr. Miraslav Tyrs—teacher, patriot, idealist—who started the physical fitness programs in the public schools. Hey, Dr. Tyrs, I'm physically fit. I wouldn't be around if I weren't. Only my sport is S and M. Would you include that in your school programs? Probably not. The folks back home seem to have gotten the sadistic part well developed. And the Blacks with their non-violence seem to be able to take it. Maybe it's not exactly masochism. I'm sure they don't look forward to being messed over. I'd hate to think of what will happen if the roles are ever reversed. And it could very well happen. There are some Blacks who don't go along with the passive-resistance ideology. Think about it. What do you gain by non-resistance? Do you make your tormentors any less violent? Are they somehow supposed to feel guilty beating on children and old ladies? It certainly hasn't produced much guilt or shame yet. Maybe now that the TV cameras catch all of this stuff on film and broadcast it, at least makes the city leaders hesitate. Bad press is bad for business—and you can't sue the media for libel when the evidence has been seen by millions around the world.

I'm going through the different museums that make up the Smithsonian. You could spend months here and not see everything. And suddenly I have a drive to see everything. Absolutely everything. I'm not sure what I will have accomplished at that point. You pass a recreational vehicle, and it has decals from every state in the Union. Is that supposed to mean something? Any more than a person who gets to know every town in his state—even if that is possible. Spending one day even in a small town doesn't get you to know what is really happening in that town. So maybe I don't have to see every piece in every exhibit. Will I have missed out on something truly important? You always miss out on something. Hell, if you get hit by a train, you might wind up missing out on your own death.

February 25, 1965

Dear Samuel,

Wheaton, Maryland. I didn't have to go far for this one. A Commemorative for Paul Revere—patriot, Revolutionary War hero. The famous ride is somehow blended in with the start of the first self-service Post Office. We are moving toward the new Revolution. The battle lines are drawn. March in Selma. Some cop shoots and kills one of the demonstrators. Things happening all over the state. One if by land, two if by sea. Cover your eyes. You can't see me.

MARCH 4, 1965

Dear Samuel,

NYC. The UN stamp commemorates the first anniversary of peacekeeping in Cyprus. Hey, guys. How about some Dutch and Danish peacekeepers in Selma? I could go for that. First anniversary of troops in Birmingham. I'd buy a whole sheet of those stamps. I would. Cyprus, by comparison, is easy. Put all the Turks on one side and all the Greeks on the other. Split the whole damned country in half. Couldn't do that here. Maybe in Birmingham. All the Blacks on one side of the tracks and all the White on the other. Put the UN troops in between. But you'd have to do that in every blasted town in the country. That would require tens of thousands of troops. Not to mention that it would be giving the racists on both sides exactly what they wanted. Total segregation. And then what do you do with the people that are mixed? In some states, a single drop of Black blood is enough to make one Black. In others, 1/32. A cool number. The same one used by the Nazis to determine that someone was Jewish and therefore candidate for extermination. And with all the plantation owners and their sons sneaking out the back door to make it with slave women, maybe all but a very few people in Dixie have at least a bit of black blood in them. Who knows, maybe even my father. That would be a joke, wouldn't it—if he found himself on the other side of the tracks. We'd need a bureaucracy in Dixie like what they have in South Africa to determine whether you were pure black or pure white or somewhere in between. That would determine where you lived, what hospital you could go to, what school, and what jobs you could get and what salaries. Come to think of it, we have most of that stuff here right now. But the tide is beginning to flow the other way. The military is fully integrated now. Black soldiers are trained the same way. Which means they know how to handle guns. And they know how to handle explosives. Somewhere along the line, if things don't start getting better, some of them might be moved to use them. I can just see the look on some Klan members' faces when their churches are bombed. When their daughters are blown to bits inside.

Hey, guys, how does it feel to be on the other side of the fence? A little S and M where you get to be the M for a change.

So . . . no UN troops on our soil—even symbolically. A recognition that to the world, our situation is no better than it is in Cyprus. I've talked to some Greeks and Turks from time to time. You should hear what they say about each other. The Turks have a museum of Greek atrocities on their side of the barrier, and the Greeks have a museum of Turkish atrocities on their side. They're all stuck in history. OK, it is a bloody history. There was a painting by a French artist early in the 19th century. I saw it in a book once. The Turks lost a battle in the Greek struggle for independence. They calculated their casualties, figured out there was an island under their control with approximately the same number of Greeks on it, and they slaughtered them all—men, women, and children. That's a history that's a bit hard to swallow. So . . . Cyprus. A wall. A clear separation. I wonder if there are some half-Greek, half-Turks. What do they do with them? A special colony? No one talks about that.

I . . . followed some girls from a middle school for a few blocks. I kept back. I was discreet. But this is getting serious. I'll have to do something about it before I get into real trouble. My fantasies are becoming really . . . obsessive.

APRIL 1, 1965

Dear Samuel,

Back in DC. What can I say? Selma. The bridge. Bloody Sunday. What will become of us? We are the pariahs of the world. I look at the pictures. In the newspapers. On TV. I hear the screams. They wake me in the middle of the night. That it should come to this. Cry. *Cry, the Beloved Country.*

A stamp—Crusade against cancer. Research. Education service.

How about the cancer that is eating our souls. Metastasizing through the body politic. This is . . . the last straw. After Selma, it is no longer possible for us to use our troops to kill our people. They are our people. They are us. Love your neighbor as yourself. Maybe that's the key. We don't even love ourselves. And we project that self-hatred onto Black people and try to kill that part of ourselves we can't face. We are killing ourselves. Bludgeoning our own mothers and fathers. Our own sisters. Our own children. How can one live with oneself after you beat a child that is on his or her knees praying to a God of justice and mercy? The same God you pray to across town. A God that will hold you accountable at the Final Trumpet—if you believe in a final judgment.

When I was growing up, they used to tell us to monitor our own behavior. What would Jesus say? What indeed? If he were in Selma, what would he say to those fine Christians who beat their fellow men on the bridge? I've seen all of this before. When will you learn, my people? When will you ever learn?

I can't go on. It's like putting salt in a bleeding sore. An ulcer that will never heal. What are people saying around town? Have they reached a breaking point? A point of no return? A point where conscience finally has its say. Tell me. I need to know. I need to know.

May 13, 1965

Dear Samuel,

I have been on the road again. I go to little towns. I eat in diners and cafes. I listen to people talking about this and that—sometimes about Selma. I just listen, hoping to hear words of disbelief—and compassion. To help me reestablish faith in the common man. Sometimes.

I am in Fulton, Missouri. In the heart of the Midwest. The stamp commemorates Winston Churchill, who died recently. He led his people through the bleakest days of the War, when German planes were bombing English towns and villages. A quote: "In War, Resolution, In Defeat, Defiance, In Victory, Magnanimity, In Peace, Goodwill." Where are we in all this? In War, in Defeat, in Victory, In Peace. Even in the Heartland of America. I can't tell. Lyndon Johnson uses the phrase "We Shall Overcome" in a speech before Congress—in an effort to pass a Civil Rights Bill over the objections of his fellow Southerners. A nice touch. We shall overcome. Perhaps. Meanwhile another martyr is added to the list—a white woman campaigning for Civil Rights in Louden County, Mississippi. Shot. Her body dumped in Big Bear Swamp. There is Southern chivalry for you, shooting an unarmed woman—a wife and mother. Something else to be proud of—to brag about to your grandchildren. Yeah, I did that. This is part of your heritage. Now go out in the world and live that down. I can't. I will hit the road again. It doesn't do much good anymore. I take all the images with me wherever I go.

May 17, 1965

Dear Samuel,

NYC. Resupply. The stamp celebrates the International Telecommunication Union. That is the only hope. Broadcast everything throughout the world. Nothing is hidden anymore. You can't do your dirty little thing and keep the world from finding out. The stories. The pictures. Maybe that will make a difference. Follow the same people from butchery to church and back to butchery. Show them in their own homes petting their dogs—maybe the same dogs they used to attack women and children. You know, Hitler was an animal lover. Some people say he was a vegetarian. It was just people he could never stand. Certain people. Watch those Southern belles cheering on the dogs. Watch their faces turn from coy and demure to savage and ugly. Focus on the children—the next generation. Another generation lost. Watch the preachers talk about the wonderful heritage they wish to preserve—and the godless heathens they say are trying to destroy it. Broadcast all this to the world. Let them snicker at our hypocrisy while they prepare to commit their own atrocities and say to themselves, "I guess we can't be all that bad if the U.S.—the supposed moral standard bearers of the world—can do such things, can permit such things to happen. Don't talk to us about Dachau and Auschwitz. Don't talk to us about Algeria or the Congo. Oh yes, we did all that. But look at Selma. Keep looking at Selma, and we don't look that way anymore. Keep those images coming from Viet Nam. There are no secrets anymore."

And yet . . . they knew about Auschwitz. Everybody knew. Roosevelt knew. Churchill knew. Hitler said everybody knew about the slaughter of the Armenians in Turkey, a mere 20 years before he started his genocidal program. It's just that nobody cared—or it was convenient to forget. Or to throw up one's hands and say that nothing could be done. So maybe here as well. Yesterday's atrocity is today's cocktail conversation. It's enough to drive a body crazy.

June 15, 1965

Dear Samuel,

I do venture South on occasion. I am in Jamestown, Virginia. I'm not sure why they picked that city to celebrate the 750th anniversary of the Magna Carta. OK, Jamestown was one of the earliest European settlements in the New World. The new charters, such as they were, included slavery. Is there a subtle connection here? Who knows? Very subtle propaganda. Too subtle for me. There are times that call for blunt truths. Hit people over the head. No time for subtle allusions.

Smalltown, USA. They finally get to put a Black man in as deputy sheriff to deal with "his" people. He is gunned down. Nothing subtle about that. Small town folk that never studied about the Magna Carta in school—and even if they had heard about it, they wouldn't make the connection nohow. Salt of the earth. Rubbing salt in the wound. I am wandering about aimlessly these days. If I didn't have these commemoratives to hold my interest, I don't know where I'd be. Not in Virginia. Not in the heart of Dixie.

JUNE 26, 1965

Dear Samuel,

I'm out West again. San Francisco. I like this place. Celebration of the UN's 20th anniversary—by the U.S. Postal Service. International Cooperation Year. The usual picture of the Secretaries-General. International cooperation. But don't focus on our internal problems. We'll handle them our own way, thank you.

Beautiful city, San Francisco—rebuilt from the ruins after the big earthquake about 60 years ago. You have to admire human resilience . . . or stubbornness—or downright stupidity. Building such a beautiful city on the same fault line, hoping that another earthquake won't happen. Blind faith. Maybe it won't happen in our generation, and once we're gone, who cares? Après moi, le deluge. A symbol of human existence. Build a city. Build a life right on the fault line. All life is precarious. Anything we build can be wiped out in a few seconds by forces beyond our control.

But that's just it. Forces beyond our control. But when the forces are in our control and we still do nothing to avert the catastrophe? That's not just blind faith. That's willful stupidity. I'd rather build my home on a fault line than on a tragic flaw. Then again, I might find as many tragic flaws here than anywhere else. I just won't stick around long enough to find them out. Just leave with pleasant memories of the town—a few good meals, the view of the ocean from up on high. And then goodbye.

July 2, 1965

Dear Samuel,

It's the 100th anniversary of the Salvation Army—its founder, General William Booth. I suppose it is something worth celebrating—people doing good work with the unfortunate, the abandoned ones, the alcoholics, drug addicts, prostitutes, and so on. I actually read some of their literature. I visited one of their shelters. Good work—at a price. Replacing one addiction for another. Religion, the opiate of the masses. But if I had a choice of heroin or alcohol and their brand of Christianity, I've freed myself from that bondage. That addiction. But what do I do with my freedom now? I haven't the slightest idea. My own blind faith is that something will hit me in my wandering. Some sudden insight—like what happened to Paul on his way to Damascus. I'm not terribly happy with what he did with that insight. At least it guided him in his wandering. He had a sense of purpose as he traveled hither and yon, preaching to the gentiles. I travel hither and yon and have next to nothing to say to anyone. Well, maybe just to you. I can write anything to you, and trust that you will make sense of it all—or if not sense, then at least you can show tolerance and compassion, maybe pity, for this poor, lost soul.

July 17, 1965

Dear Samuel,

The 700th birthday of the Italian poet Dante. A bit of appreciation for great literature. Dante. The Inferno. Purgatorio, Paradiso. Where are we in the process? Are we out of Hell yet? Maybe, in the first two circles of Purgatory, where we pay for our sins, that we gain some hope for atonement and absolution. The opening of the Equal Employment Opportunity Commission. A glimmer of hope. A sense of direction. Again, the Feds. Not clear that anything on the Federal level will penetrate the Mason-Dixon Line. There are certain people I would feel good about knowing that they were roasting in Hell. Eternal damnation. If I believed in that.

It's hard in the absence of justice here on earth not to at least hope for a Final Judgment somewhere at some time. If death is final, who cares if one is Hitler or a saint? It all comes to the same thing. Ecclesiastes. The same problem. If everybody winds up the same, why not indulge in wine, women, and song? I'm not much on wine. Not much into singing these days. Women are another matter. Finding a woman who can tickle my fancy. Not just play at it—indulge my fantasy and find it . . . meaningful. Strange way to find meaning in life. Plunge into the heart of darkness—free oneself and then project the horror onto the world. The rain in my heart that inundates the world.

AUGUST 4, 1965

Dear Samuel,

I'm in Newberry Port, Mass. The 175th anniversary of the U.S. Coast Guard—protecting our coasts from our enemies. We have met the enemy, and they are us. Nothing the Coast Guard can do about that. They can save a boat in a storm. But when the storm rages inland. When it rages inside the individual and the collective soul? What then? What then, Big Ben? Ask not for whom the bell tolls. It tolls for you. Tones. Intones. Bemoans. Can these bones live again? Hearts of stone. Uncircumcised hearts. Sinners in the hands of a vengeful God. Would that it were so.

AUGUST 19, 1965

Dear Samuel,

The 200th anniversary of the steamboat. Robert Fulton sails from NYC to Albany. Fitting. The President steers the Ship of State through the Voting Rights Act. It's now Federal law. We'll see how much difference the law makes.

There are riots going on in Los Angeles. Race Riots. Our steamship coming home to roost. Philadelphia, Harlem, Los Angeles. It doesn't matter where you are. The flames are creeping close. Hearts inflamed. It just takes one spark. There are sparks flying everywhere. Tinder everywhere. Beware. I don't care. Do you dare. The flare. Your hair. The old grey mare. We don't have a prayer. Brother can you spare—a match. Beware.

AUGUST 28, 1965

Dear Samuel,

The 400th anniversary of the founding of St. Augustine. By Pedro Mendez de Aviles. A Spaniard. The first permanent European settlement in what was to become the U.S. I'm not sure the Seminoles are celebrating. The city named for St. Augustine. I'm not sure why. OK, he wrote about forming a heavenly city, based on Christian principles, as he saw them. He lived a riotous life in his youth. Then a sudden conversion—like St. Paul. I don't like him much better. The Heavenly city, where babies that die before they're baptized go to Hell. He called that one of the Divine mysteries. Spare us from such mysteries. His Hell included all pagans—native Americans, I suppose, had he known about them, so why not help them fulfill their destiny a bit faster. You could proselytize, but that didn't preclude slavery or massacre when it was convenient.

Interesting that he came from the same town as Santa Teresa. Now that was an interesting woman. Celibate to be sure. (Where does the Church get that? The first commandment in the Bible is to be fruitful and multiply.) But when she writes about her mystic encounter with the Holy Spirit—or one of the Archangels—the language is sexual, bordering on the masochistic. I have a few fantasies about that myself. Naughty thoughts. The woman had a rich fantasy life. A roaring libido. You ever see a picture of Bernini's statue of Santa Teresa? Best statue of a woman having an orgasm that I've ever seen. A bride of Christ. Bernini has her fully clothed. I suppose that was the only decent thing he could do. Can you have an orgasm fully clothed? I suppose so. A Divine orgasm as the angel plunges his arrow into her breast time after time. The joints of the thigh—twin breasts like two fawns, etc. The holy etcetera as Cummings would put it. My mind wanders. I won't wander too far afield. Not down into Florida. Not if I have to go through the Carolinas and Georgia to get there. You'll have to get this one on your own.

SEPTEMBER 3, 1965

Dear Samuel,

I'm in Baltimore. A stamp promoting traffic safety. Why in Baltimore of all places? Some things are not worth speculating about. Like the origin of the universe. The origin of life. The reason for my existence. The drive for traffic safety in Baltimore. Curiouser and curiouser.

I suppose I should be careful of how I drive in Baltimore. I'm not sure why. But I don't think I'm ready to leave this earth in a fiery crash on the streets of Baltimore. Some unknown visitor to the city—with no family or friends. Not enough money to bury him in style. A pauper's grave. Forgotten by all but . . . God?

SEPTEMBER 20, 1965

Dear Samuel,

Back in NYC. The UN stamp honors the memory of Dag Hammerskjold. I really have to look up his biography. Why was he so honored?

Two Black students enroll in the University of Southern Mississippi. The world doesn't fall apart. Is this the beginning of the millennium? A program on TV with a Black co-star. A popular program. I'll have to check it out. Is it really possible, and if so, what is next? Television ads showing Black parents wondering what breakfast cereal to feed their kids, what kind of laundry detergent to use to make their linens really white, what kind of soap to use to get rid of body odor. The Revolution has begun, I tell you. Bull Connor be damned. Governor Wallace as well. Your battle is over. Appomattox. Hang it up. The next thing you know, there will be Black quarterbacks playing for the University of Alabama. And you all will be in the stands cheering in spite of yourselves. Look at that Injun heave that pigskin. Isn't it just grand?

October 6, 1965

Dear Samuel,

The 100th anniversary of the International Telecommunications Union. Honoring Alexander Bell and Samuel F. B. Morse. Things have progressed a bit since then. At least the technology. We can see the carnage of war in Viet Nam in real time—the villages burning, the violence in Selma. I suppose that's progress of a sort. It would be nice to see people planting forests in Malaysia or saving wildlife in Brazil, but you can't have everything. Nobody wants to see the good stuff. You don't go to a car race to see everybody toodling along without an incident. That's just boring. There needs to be a crash or two. That's what everyone is waiting for. Cars spinning in the air, wheels flying this way and that—and fire. It's OK if the drivers get out unscathed. For some people, that's just fine. Others want to see the ambulances carry off the wounded. That's what we pay good money to see. Mayhem. That's why the Romans went to the Coliseum. The civilized Romans. Watch Christians be fed to the lions. Watch the gladiators hack each other to death. That's why Spaniards go to bullfights. The anticipation of blood and gore. That's why people go to watch boxing. The primitive part of our psyches. Show us the gore. Blood galore. It doesn't really matter whose, as long as we can remain spectators. As long as it's someone else's blood that is splattered. Three cheers for Mr. Bell. New technology. Old taste for blood.

October 21, 1965

Dear Samuel,

Philadelphia. Pennsylvania, not Mississippi. The stamp honors the Bureau of the Census. Why in mid-decade? They won't be taking the census for another four and a half years. Way back when they took the first census, Blacks counted for only 3/5. That was not because the South thought Blacks were 60% human. They just wanted to maximize their political clout in the House of Representatives. You can't do that anymore. And now Blacks can actually vote. And they're not likely to vote for the likes of a Bull Connor. I read somewhere about Marcus Garvey back in the '20s. He was talking about Africa. How once the nations there became independent and in control of their own natural resources, the Europeans that once called Africans "boy" would now call them "sir." I can just see it. All those politicians kowtowing to Blacks to get their votes. There may yet come a day when Black politicians canvas to get White votes. Or is that too much of a fantasy on my part. I have a lot of fantasies these days—not all of them political. I wonder how many categories in the next Census will deal with fantasies? Sexual fantasies. Isn't there someone in Indiana who is studying such fantasies? A Dr. Kinsey. I heard that he originally studied the sex life of insects. Gregor Mendel woke up one morning and found that he had been turned into a giant cockroach. It has come to that. To the giants, Gulliver looked like a bug. The female mantis eats her mate during copulation. The spies in Canaan felt like grasshoppers. Black widows eat their mates. Maybe it's just civilization that covers over the natural impulses we have. Maybe we're just bugs of a higher order.

October 23, 1965

Dear Samuel,

Bloomington, Illinois. I wanted to make sure I got here in time. A stamp honoring Adlai Stevenson—distinguished citizen, Governor, Ambassador to the UN. I wouldn't have minded seeing him as President of the U.S. But he was too intellectual—too uncharismatic to win over a military hero. You heard some of his speeches. He appealed to the intellect. To reason. You knew that would never fly. No one can get elected in this country by appealing to people's reason. To their gut, yes. To their minds, give it up. The stamp is a good likeness. There may yet come a time when a true statesman can become the leader of a great nation. But take England. You get a man like Churchill. He led his nation through the horrors of the War. He inspired his people with the will to survive. And then, as soon as the War was over, he was ousted from office. The people spoke. They showed their gratitude. Was it de Tocqueville who wrote about us that we didn't want true leaders? Just men who reflected our mediocrity. These days I would settle for mediocrity. Just as long as the mediocrity led us slowly in the right direction. Some sense of leadership, not just floundering. Hiding in the sand with our eyes exposed to notice what is going back and forth in the water above.

An executive order requiring Equal Opportunity by Federal contractors. That's big. Not big enough. The Feds get to fund a lot of projects that require the hiring of a lot of workers. But if the contractors don't take any Federal money, they can be as prejudiced as they please. States' rights. I'm sure that some smart-assed lawyers will find some way to get some of the contracts to fall under Federal jurisdiction. We will drag some people into the modern world kicking and screaming. Let them kick and scream until their energy flags. Sometimes it's not justice that prevails. It's the ones that can hold out the longest. Not justice, but stamina. Fortitude. Stubbornness. Stubbornness in the name of justice. Most people just give up after a few half-hearted efforts. Like parents who give in to the demands of their children, especially if they throw a tantrum or two. I'm glad I don't have any children. At least none that I am aware of. I don't think I would have the stamina. That's it. A lack of stamina. Fortitude. A sense of purpose. Blacks outlasting the stubbornness of the Yahoos with a little help from the Feds. I'm just a butterfly of sorts flitting from flower to flower, never staying in any one place for very long. Getting just a nip of sweetness here and there. At best. And then moving on. Always. Moving on.

OCTOBER 25, 1965

Dear Samuel,

Back in NYC. Stamp from the UN. Self-defined purpose. Idealistic. We, the people of the UN, determined to save succeeding generations from the scourge of war. Sounds good. I don't know how many wars have been prevented in the past 25 years. The way the UN is set up, any nation can block any resolution that comes before the Security Council. If the Soviet Union wants to invade a country, it can just veto any measure that condemns its actions. If one of the Allies commits atrocities on its own people, it can label its actions as an internal situation, beyond the reach of the UN. Like in the U.S.—States' rights. Not under Federal jurisdiction, except when things get so bad, the Feds will find some way to intervene. I suppose the UN can exert some muscle with small nations that don't have much clout. Be thankful for small things. Let the big stuff go. A weird philosophy to maintain. Let the Nazis and the Soviets perpetuate atrocities on a grand scale. Save the Tahitians, the Samoans, the Montenegrins, the Patagonians from their misadventures. It's the best that we can do.

November 2, 1965

Dear Samuel,

I'm tired. I don't want to cross the country again. Stamp in Silver Bell, Arizona. I don't even know what it's about. I find myself saying I don't care anymore. In a bit of a deep funk. You can get the envelope from a dealer. I'll deal with the funk somehow.

November 9, 1965

Dear Samuel,

The stamp shows the image of Lincoln—the ASDA National Postage Stamp Show. Are there dealers from Dixie who will protest because it's Lincoln? Let them protest. I don't give a damn anymore. What the Hell! They lost the War. Then. And now. We lost the War. Get over it. I feel . . . lost. Like I lost some war I didn't even know I was fighting, let alone who the enemy was. Is. We have met the enemy, and they are us. I talked with someone who was into karate. Big time. Black belt. Could break bricks and boards with his bare hands. He could put an untrained assailant on his back in a matter of seconds. Kill him if necessary. You know what all this training is about? He asked me. I shook my head. We are preparing to meet the ultimate enemy in the dark of night. Who is the greatest enemy? I asked him. You know the answer already, he told me. And I did. The greatest enemy is just ourselves. He is preparing for that fight. I am not. Just hoping the struggle will not come. I will be defeated when it does. I will pay for that lack of preparation. I will pay dearly.

NOVEMBER 29, 1965

Dear Samuel,

Did I miss the Christmas stamp this year? Was it the one in Arizona? I'm getting forgetful in my old age. Sloppy. Sorry. The new UN stamp commemorates Population Trends Development, whatever that means. Probably trying to stem the population explosion in the Third World. Some nations are doubling their population every 16 years in spite of high levels of infant mortality. So . . . we feel sorry for them. Go in and bring medicine to save their children. Can't talk to them about birth control. That would be imposing our values on their culture. Even in our country. So many Catholics. The Pope. Let God take care of the problem. Let conception happen as it will. So the babies don't die in utero. They just get born, are malnourished, and die later. Or don't die. Live a life of squalor and desperation and produce children of their own. God's will. Sure. Malthus. Food production increases arithmetically, population geometrically. Go figure. The degree of human misery increases geometrically. God's will. As if we were not given a brain to figure things out. God's will be damned! Man fashions God to reinforce the craziest ideas he can come up with. The Big Endians vs. the Little Endians. The Right Footians vs. the Left Footians. Two sides fighting each other, killing each other over such stupid stuff. Does the Bread and Wine actually become the Body and Blood—are they co-existent, or is it all symbolic? Certainly reason enough to start a Holy War. I am sick of all this stuff. Sick . . . and tired. The year is coming to an end. Good riddance. No hope that things will be any better in the year to come.

JANUARY 29, 1966

Dear Samuel,

I just don't know how the time passes. I can't even remember how I spent the holidays. Christmas. New Year's. It's all a fog. Where was I yesterday? Did I sell those three carpets or just give them away? The woman I was with. The woman. And how did I get this tattoo on my arm? The rose with thorns dripping blood—underneath Gothic letters spelling out the word PAIN.

I am in Hyde Park, NY. The hangout of FDR. Part of the Prominent American Series. FDR. The first President to use the radio to speak directly to the public—his fireside chats, the illusion of keeping them informed about the working of their government. The illusion that their opinions counted for something in the deliberation process.

Another Civil Rights leader killed in Hattiesburg, Mississippi. I suppose that every cause must have its martyrs. Someone said, it's not a real principle in your life if you are not willing to die for it. I guess I'm not willing to die just yet. Not just yet.

The President says that neither old wrongs or new fears can justify arson or murder. Wait. I can't hear you. Just the screams of Vernon Dahmer as he is blown to bits in Hattiesburg. I can't hear you, Mr. President. I can't hear anything you have to say.

January 31, 1966

Dear Samuel,

The UN again. Twentieth Anniversary of the Federation of UN Associations. Associations of Associations. Celebration of their mere existence. No purpose. Like ads for a food that is popular but has no known nutritional value.

MATCH 16, 1966

Dear Samuel,

Pittsburgh. The 50th anniversary of the Migratory Bird Treaty between the U.S. and Canada. The envelope shows the summer nesting area of the whooping crane. Almost extinct. Barely hanging on. All that effort to keep a few species from dying out. What would the world be like without whooping cranes? Without dodos and passenger pigeons. Dodos. Trusting souls. Walked right up to wandering sailors and got clubbed to death. Couldn't fly. A face so ugly only a mother could love it. Only a mother, had she survived. She didn't. Extinct. Extinct is forever. Once you're dead, you're dead. Forever. Oblivion. No treaty can prevent that.

MATCH 25, 1966

Dear Samuel,

NYC. The Pope visits the UN. Offers a prayer for peace. Commemorated with a one-dollar stamp. I guess if you're the Pope, you can get such an honor. A one-dollar stamp. You can send a lot through the mail for a dollar. Pope Paul VI. Was he a good Pope? Was his prayer worth anything at all? A prayer. I don't have a prayer. No stamps for me.

APRIL 9, 1966

Dear Samuel,

NYC. Stamp for the Humane Treatment of Animals. Cats. A child and a puppy. It appeals to the heart. Don't appeal to the Governor. He won't comply with the orders of the President to integrate public schools. Can't make him. Nya nya nya nya nya. Your mother wears army boots. Your father shaves his legs.

You know there was a law banning cruelty to animals before there was a law preventing cruelty to children? You could do just about anything you wanted to your own children, but you'd better not beat your horse in public. Naughty, naughty. Make nice to your horse. String up a nigga for being uppity. Beat your wife. Nice stamp. Nice stamp. Pulls at your heartstrings. Where exactly are the heartstrings? I didn't learn that in biology class. Didn't learn much of anything at all.

April 16, 1966

Dear Samuel,

On the road again. Indiana, Corydon. The first state courthouse was built here 150 years ago. The first state Governor was John Jennings, in case you wanted to know. I suppose if you were a student in Indiana, you would have to learn the names of all of the Governors. A lot of names. You might have to learn the name of the Governor in 1928, who ran with the Klan. Keep Catholics out of public office. Out of the Presidency. Catholics have dual loyalty—to the Constitution of the U.S. and to the Vatican. Whereas the Klan obviously was made up of true, loyal Americans—everyone. Good white Protestant Americans. Protecting the country from subversives—like Catholics, kikes, and niggers. I have to keep reminding myself that this is Indiana, not Mississippi—the sun never set on a nigger in this town. The only thing lower than a nigger is a migrant worker from Kentucky. You should hear the stories they tell of Kentucky folk.

I can't marry your daughter, Clem.

Why not?

Have you slept with her yet?

Nope.

Well, if she ain't good enough for you, she ain't good enough for me nohow.

There are unincorporated company towns here where the company owns the schools, the churches, the banks, the post office. Makes whatever rules it wants to. No unions. No nothing. And this is whites dealing with whites. Indiana folk putting down Kentucky folk, for God's sakes—as if Indiana folk had a mandate from Heaven and Kentucky folk were the spawn of Ham, condemned to servitude for all eternity. So you can still go to church and feel right with God and then go out and treat people from south of the border worse then you treat your own dog. Hitler treated his dogs well. And he was a vegetarian. I read that once. Did I tell you that already? I forget.

May 2, 1966

Dear Samuel,

Delavan, Wisconsin. Salute to the American Circus. John Ringling. The Ringing Brothers. Happy clowns. Clowns are either happy or sad—nothing in between. I saw a show once—Marcel Marceau. Where? I can't remember. He is a clown. Sad. He tries on a mask. It has a happy face on it. He takes it off. Sad again. Puts it back on. Happy. Tries to get it off again. Can't. It's stuck. The smile is fixed. The body shows despair. Anguish. That's me. Trapped in an invisible cage. I claw my way here and there—finally discover an opening. I squeeze through. Brief moments of elation. Then I discover that I'm in another box with no apparent opening. And even if there were an opening, there would certainly be another box. And yet another box. Invisible. And yet as confining as if it were made of brick and stone. One small window with bars. Will I ever get to play in an open field again? Under the sun. How can I prove my innocence? With each step I take, I prove my own guilt. Even for life itself. For breathing. Every day one step closer to the executioners who pass the knife back and forth between them, waiting for me to take it from them. To act like a man. To do the job myself. Act like a man. Not like a clown.

MAY 21, 1966

Dear Samuel,

DC. The International Philatelic Society Exhibition. Pretty pieces of colored paper behind glass cases. Stuff people collect. Like first day issues. Like buckshot in the back. How do you like that collection, James? How do you like that, boy? You think you're hot stuff, on a one-man March against Fear from Memphis to Jackson. You think you're hot shit—that one nigger can change the world. The world loves martyrs. Rally to the cause. Well, bird shot is cheap. Everybody in Mississippi that's worth anything carries a shotgun in his pickup truck. At least the Whites do. Heaven help us if the niggers ever got a notion to do the same. I can see my father sporting a few pellets in his back. Well, I'll be damned, he'd say. To think of a nigger sporting a shotgun. And having the temerity to aim it at a white man. God's chosen people. What in the tarnation is this world coming to?

I went to the Convention. Not a Blackman in sight. It figures. Not too many stamp collectors in the Congo or in Bangladesh. Got to know where your next meal is coming from before you worry about plateblocks and watermarks.

JULY 1, 1966

Dear Samuel,

In Miami. The stamp commemorates the 175th anniversary of the Bill of Rights. You'll have to get that one on your own.

Some radicals stomping around Civil Rights meetings talking about Black Power. Answering violence with violence. No more Gandhi. No more non-violent resistance. Appealing to the conscience of Whites. Maybe you could do that in India with the British. Even in a place like Nigeria. But it doesn't work with Rednecks. They're another breed. Like a bulldog that bites you and just hangs on until you shoot him in the head. Even then you might have to pry his jaws apart.

A bulldog. Like the President. A bit of a surprise. The folks in Mississippi and Alabama didn't count on dealing with a country boy from Texas. Don't mess with Texas. With Texans. Civil Rights Bill sent to Congress banning discrimination in the sale or rental of houses everywhere in the U.S. Good politics. You can't say now that he was just targeting the South. You know how many neighborhoods I've seen up here that won't sell or rent to Blacks? To Jews for that matter—or even to Italians. He's pushing for legislature to end discrimination in the selection of federal and state juries. I'm not sure he can pull that one off. Aren't you supposed to be judged by a panel of your peers? And if you're a Klansman, doesn't that mean a jury of Klansmen? There's a proposed law to initiate suits by the Attorney General to force integration of public facilities. Don't we have that law in the books already? Isn't this just spitting in the wind? Pissing in the urinal. Even if he managed to get all that enacted into law, what would change? King talks about changing men's hearts. It won't happen in my lifetime. Not in my children's lifetimes, supposing that I had any. Maybe I do. I might go wandering someplace into some town, and somebody would come up to me with open arms, shouting, "Daddy!" That would be a pisser, wouldn't it? What could they demand of me? Half of my rug inventory? My collection of sex toys? Let me play parent at long last. Teach them everything I've learned in my life. That should take about five minutes at most.

July 30, 1966

Dear Samuel,

DC. The stamp commemorates 1,000 years of Polish culture. Some people might say that the expression Polish culture is a contradiction in terms. All those Polack jokes. How can you tell who is the bride at a Polack wedding? She's the one with the clean undershirt, or she's the one with braided underarm hair. I shouldn't repeat all that. As the saying goes, some of my best friends are Polacks. If I had any best friends. At least around here.

Between Pittsburgh and Chicago, you can tune into stations that play Polish music. Mostly Polkas. There's culture for you. What Poland gave to the world. The Polka. The Mazurka. And there were some scientists back a ways. Wasn't Kepler Polish? He placed us in orbit around the sun, not in the center of the universe. So. No more Polish jokes. Who knows how many Polish painters there were? Novelists, playwrights, poets. Maybe even philosophers. Every culture deserves a commemorative to honor what it has contributed to the world. Why a 1,000 years? The first king of Poland. Let's hear it for Prince Mieccyslaw I and Boleslaw I. They ruled over territory between Russia and Germany. What land is actually Poland today? How many people live there? There might be more Polish-speaking people between Chicago and Pittsburgh.

Ah, Chopin. He was Polish. Of course he spent nearly all of his adult life in Paris. I remember hearing the Revolutionary Etude. I think Chopin would have given up his life in Paris—all the women that flocked about him—if he could have picked up a rifle and fought for Polish independence. If he weren't so consumptive—so wrapped up in performances and liaisons. No non-violence there. But he stayed in France—bleeding internally, as it were—in exile, from a distance. Sounds familiar. Only I can't play the piano. I can't compose a note. No excuses. I don't have TB. I'm not being fawned over by a bevy of highborn, rich ladies. Or even a bluestocking or two like George Sand. She must have been something. Wonder what it would be like to kiss a woman whose breath smelled from cigars. Women are adaptable. They have to be.

The President says that 60% of the Southern and border schools have complied with the Civil Rights Act of 1964. Not bad for starters. What does it mean at this point? One or two black faces in each school? I hear tell a lot of cities are pushing for private schools now. White flight. In a few years, all the public schools will be all-black again. Maybe not all. Maybe there is such a thing as progress. What was unthinkable yesterday becomes what is normal tomorrow. How do you like dem apples, Governor Wallace. You sleeping pretty well these days?

AUGUST 25, 1966

Dear Samuel,

Leisurely trip out West. Everything I do these days seems to be in slow motion. One might think that would help me remember where I've been. But I don't. I can't tell you what towns I've been through en route to Yellowstone National Park—to celebrate the 50th anniversary of the National Park Service. Was that created during the Presidency of Teddy Roosevelt? Conserve the scientific, scenic, and historic heritage for the benefit and enjoyment of the people of the United States. A noble ideal. Most of the people I see here are white. Overwhelmingly. So maybe the message hasn't gone out to non-whites that the Park is here for them too. Maybe they're a bit preoccupied these days. Black power advocates rival the more traditional groups for membership. Riots break out in Omaha, Chicago, Brooklyn, Jacksonville, and Cleveland. The President says that the street riots don't bring about lasting reform. They tear the very fabric of the community. They set neighbor against neighbor and create walls of distrust and fear. They alienate the very people that might be inclined to favor reform. And the destruction that ensues affects Blacks disproportionately.

All that sounds rational, except that most change doesn't come about rationally. You create fear—present a rational agenda, and then the public turns in desperation to the very moderates they ignored before. And then the moderates up the ante—secretly grateful for the actions of the radicals, whose tactics the public eschews. That's how things get done in the world. Maybe it shouldn't be that way, but it is. There was a political theorist writing about 40 years ago on how you manipulate public opinion through fear and anxiety. Mussolini thought his ideas were brilliant—Machiavellian. It's OK for a Prince to lie—to use propaganda, as long as he doesn't wind up believing his own lies. That's the problem, though, with most dictators. They are so preoccupied with self-glorification, they come to believe in their own lies. Hitler. Stalin. They all fell in the same trap. And millions of people paid for their stupidity.

It's not like that here. You see bears ambling by. Bears don't lie. If they want to attack you, they don't spread stories about how it's all for your own good or for the good of the nation. They just go for you unapologetically and rip at your flesh. I've walked a few trails. I've seen a few bears. Been tempted to rush at them. They say that bears are intimidated by such bravado. Or, on the other hand, they defend their territory and go on the attack. Strange feelings. On the one hand, I think it would feel good being able to intimidate a creature that weighs in at a thousand pounds or more—which can rear up to a height of eight or nine feet and could crush my skull with one swipe of its paw or one bite of its jaws. On the other hand, a part of me wouldn't resist an attack—wouldn't fight back. Somehow it would seem preferable to be dispatched by a bear rather than by a person—a cop or a mugger. Better claws and teeth than knives, guns, or a lead pipe. I'm getting a bit foolhardy in my behavior. Bear. Moose. I haven't seen any rattlesnakes yet. That might be OK. Lying on some deserted path, the poison coursing through my veins. I read up on rattlesnakes yesterday. There should be plenty of them around here. I haven't seen one.

September 12, 1966

Dear Samuel,

I managed to survive Yellowstone. I seem to lead a charmed life. Back in NYC. The stamp honors the General Federation of Women's Clubs on their 75th anniversary. The founder was Jennie June Crotty. That puts the organization back at a time before women got the vote. Prophetic. Women celebrating common interests in philanthropy, public welfare, moral values in education, civics, and the fine arts. Image of women in typical dress then and now. I ought to study the women's movement. Things don't change over the years. They were mocked for wanting to vote—for wanting to become doctors and, horrors, for wanting to run for public office. That would rock the very foundation of society—produce instability. Women should know their place—in the kitchen, in the bedroom, in the nursery. Look at the Bible, how women are praised in Ecclesiastes—St. Paul establishing that men should rule the household and women should obey. Sound familiar? White men telling women to accept subservience joyfully as a God-given station in life, like the curse of Ham. You gave Adam the apple, you get to pay for that for all eternity. Convenient. An obviously male God putting the woman in her place. How dare anyone challenge that? It would be impious. Irreverent. Blasphemous. Sacrilegious. And yet women did get the vote. They did become doctors. They did run for office. And the world is still here. God didn't rain down fire and brimstone. Maybe God is female. Maybe God is a Black woman and she is pissed at us for our impiety in maintaining the status quo.

Or maybe God just isn't and we've got to do all this on our own just because it's the right thing to do—and it's better to be just than unjust. We hold these principles to be self-evident, that all men are created equal and they are endowed with certain inalienable rights—life, liberty, and the pursuit of happiness. Shouldn't what is self-evident be self-evident? Wasn't this the basis on which the country was founded? The bottom line for anyone who calls himself an American? Am I the only one crazy enough to believe this? Well, maybe not the only one. Surely not the only one. Surely . . . not.

September 19, 1966

Dear Samuel,

NYC still. Picked up some new carpets. Really nice stuff. Some new toys. New stuff. The use of intellect in the service of the libido.

The UN celebrates the Coffee Agreement. An effort to balance supply and demand. Picture of a woman picking the beans and a man processing them. Third world types. The agreement probably benefits the developed nations that control supply and demand rather than the peasant types that actually work the fields and produce the marketable product. It is always like this. The rich want a predictable product at what they would consider to be a reasonable price. If that means keeping thousands of workers at subsistent-level pay, so be it. Anything so that we in the developed world can get our morning cup of coffee. How could I get through the day without coffee? The whole world would collapse. The peasants are simple folk. They probably couldn't handle a raise in their wages. They would probably buy booze and beat on their wives, so we are doing them a favor keeping them down-trodden. They should thank us for understanding their needs so well.

September 24, 1966

Dear Samuel,

Leominster, Mass. Check a map. The stamp celebrates the legendary Johnny Appleseed—John Chapman, who went around planting fruit trees all around Pennsylvania, Ohio, Indiana, and Illinois. He lived from 1775 to 1847. A good long life back then—living in the open air. Plenty of exercise. A real sense of purpose. I can't quite relate the dates of his life to the date of the stamp. The 191st anniversary of his birth, the 119th anniversary of his death.

Interesting controversy about him you don't usually hear about. A lot of the trees he planted did not produce good eating apples. It turned out people used the fruit for making cider. Hard cider. That was the booze of choice in many communities. It was cheap. You could make it yourself. The temperance ladies got up in arms and went around chopping down a lot of the trees Mr. Chapman had planted. History isn't always tidy. We remember what we think of as being convenient to remember. I could use a swig of cider about now. Strong cider.

Same town. Same day. Stamp honoring the U.S. Marine Resource Corps. Picture of Marines in action—helicopter, boats staging a landing. There should be boats in the picture, shouldn't there? They are called Marines. Weird to have two stamps issued the same day in the same place. Is there a hidden message here? We are currently fighting a war. Have an apple. Have a mug of cider. Get plastered. Our Marines are dying, fighting half-way around the world—a war that doesn't make sense to a lot of people, considering all the crap that's happening here in the U.S. So let's celebrate Johnny Appleseed. Take your mind off things. An apple a day keeps the shrink away. I tried it. An apple a day. Doesn't quite work for me.

October 21, 1966

Dear Samuel,

No, I'm not in Baton Rouge. The stamp celebrates the Great River Road—a scenic route from Canada to the Gulf of Mexico. I saw the stamp. No need to go to Baton Rouge. You can get it from a dealer.

Ironic. Canada to the Gulf of Mexico. The opposite direction from the Underground Railroad. They haven't honored that yet with a stamp. Maybe the road wasn't all that scenic.

News from California. The founding of a group that calls itself the Black Panthers. Doesn't exactly sound like a group that preaches non-violence. Some stormy times ahead. Interesting mascot. Color phase of a leopard. Their attack mode—hide out in trees and jump on a person's back as you pass. Somewhat sinister. Leopards are known to be maneaters. Ambush killers. They attack mostly at night. Think about that for a while. Think. Think. Think.

October 24, 1966

Dear Samuel,

UN. Honoring Peacekeepers. Vigil for Peace. Preventing flare-ups. Elsewhere. Blessed be the Peacekeepers. Where are the Peacekeepers? Not in Brooklyn—just across the river. Not in LA. Keeping the pieces together. Half the times I feel fragmented. Torn. Shorn. Jimmy cracks corn, and I don't care. My massah's gone away. Forlorn. Worn. Unborn. How do I keep myself together? I sell porn.

OCTOBER 26, 1966

Dear Samuel,

I raced halfway across the country. I barely slept. Sioux City, Iowa. The 25th anniversary of U.S. Savings Bond. In 1941, DR issued the Bonds to help raise money for the war effort. The Bonds were signed by the Secretary of the Treasury, Henry Morgenthau Jr. Appropriate. I think he was Jewish. Help fight the Nazis. You have to trust the stability of the country to pay you back with interest. Do the patriotic thing. I remember as a child buying a stamp that would add up to a Bond. You paid $18 and got back $25 some years down the road. I don't remember what happened to my bonds. I don't remember cashing them in. It was easy to be patriotic back then. We were fighting the Huns. If they managed to win the War, they would come and rape our women. Them and the Japanese. We put Japanese-Americans into prison camps and concentration camps. We didn't go so far as to gas them. But by the time we let them out, their property was gone. We never did that to German-Americans or Italian-Americans. Maybe that was racial. Then again, Eisenhower was a descendant of German immigrants. So there. Where? Maybe we sent Japanese-Americans to fight the Germans and German-Americans to fight the Japanese. I don't know. We're at War again for a change. Good propaganda to portray the enemy as brutes—semi-human. Of course we would never behave the way they do. We're civilized.

November 1, 1966

Dear Samuel,

Christmas stamp. Religious image. Madonna, child, and angels by Messing. The town is called Christmas. I don't feel much holiday cheer. You can get that stamp on your own. Funny. The Post Office keeps putting out Christmas images on stamps. Are we a Christian nation? Where do Jews and Hindus fit in—let alone atheists? What kind of stamp would you issue to acknowledge the atheists among us? Maybe a stamp that was completely black—or blank. That would be wild.

NOVEMBER 28, 1966

Dear Samuel,

Back in NYC. Twentieth anniversary of UNICEF. The stamps show children of all colors playing together on a toy train. The artist dressed them to look African, Latino, Asian, and European. The envelope touts the organization's aid to governments to develop free public education. I would imagine it would be integrated. On one stamp the children are on a wagon with no truck to drive them. On another there is a black boy dressed as a doctor and a white girl dressed as a nurse. Interesting. Maybe there should be an alternate stamp with a white woman as the doctor and the black man as the nurse. Or a black woman as the doctor and a white man as the nurse. Manipulate the images a bit. White woman with a food basket or let the black woman give food to a white child. Surely there must be some black philanthropists and some needy white children. Stereotypes. Even when people try to free themselves from prejudice and do the right thing, the stereotypes persist. Some of them are beginning to break down. Black Panthers on the prowl. No more happy Negroes singing spirituals on the plantation. Funny thing. I like spirituals. Maybe not the plantations. Could you have one without the other? Go down, Moses. Joshua fit the battle of Jericho. And dee walls come tumbling down. They had a vision back then. They hid it pretty cleverly. They're not hiding it anymore. If the walls don't come tumbling down, they're going to burn them down. And we're going to sit around and wonder what happened to the people we thought we knew so well.

Hey, they elected a Black man to the U.S. Senate from Massachusetts. The first Black Senator in 85 years. OK, he's from Massachusetts. Yankee County. Now if he were to be elected in Alabama, that would really be something. Maybe in two years. Ho, ho, ho.

But they did hire one Black cop in Birmingham. One. Count him. And two Black dentists got accepted into the Birmingham Dental Association. Two. Wow! By the end of the century, who knows, maybe a Black Mayor. Even a Black President. I should live so long. Maybe even a Black woman.

January 23, 1967

Dear Samuel,

Still in NYC. Masses of people celebrating the coming of the New Year. I wonder why. Do they really think it will be any better than the last? Hope springs eternal in the human breast.

Hope. Raw courage. Julian Bond is seated in the Georgia House of Representatives by order of the U.S. Supreme Court. It still takes the Feds to make democracy work in Dixie. Then again, where there's a will, there's a way. I suppose democracy is at work in Alabama too. George Wallace couldn't run for another term as Governor. So his wife ran for him, and most of the voters said that was fine. You can imagine who will run the state. I heard someone quip, "In Alabama bedfellows make strange politics." Not strange for Alabama. Business as usual.

A bunch of stamps from the UN. Some tout the Development Programme. Is that British English? It's not the way I learned to spell it in school. Development. Applying research techniques to tackle agriculture problems in the World Wide War on hunger. I can tell you the source of hunger in parts of Alabama and Mississippi, and it has nothing to do with agriculture. Job training. I don't know how much training it takes to be a ticket taker on a train—or a Pullman coachman. A janitor. A tenant farmer. That almost exhausts the possibilities for some—unless they work for a Federal agency like the Post Office or they volunteer for the military. Of course then you get to be shot at halfway around the world by Viet Cong snipers who are equal-opportunity snipers. They don't care if the American they kill is Black or White.

Another stamp commemorates the Peace Bell Japan gave to the UN. I can understand why they would want peace 22 years after we killed those tens of thousands of people with A bombs and poisoned the survivors with radiation. What I can't understand about the Japanese is how they put their supposed love of peace and their Kamikaze war tactics together. Meditate in a Zen garden. Write a few Haiku poems. Contemplate a floral arrangement or a Brush painting. And then get into a plane and dive bomb enemy ships or civilian populations in China, take a few thousand Korean women to be sex slaves, force enemy POWs to go on a death march. How does all this fit together? I can't even put the parts of my own psyche together. My fascination with both S and M—in an instant moving from perpetrator to victim and back again with a person who tells me that she and I are truly partners. Yes, I found my "friend" again. She had nothing to do to end the year. No better partner. We spent the holiday week doing what seems to come naturally to us. Or maybe not naturally. Maybe it's all coming from the mind. But isn't human behavior natural for human beings? Kinsey described all kinds of things people do—behaviors many would call perverse or abnormal. But if a large number of people—even a majority—do it, can it be unnatural, perverse, sinful? I am not a philosopher. I think about the brain. The mind. Two centuries ago, one philosopher traced what looked like strange behavior to the influence of what today we would call hormones. Maybe everything we can think up to do is in some sense natural. Or maybe none of it is natural. Somewhere along the line we stepped off the Nature train and are in some exotic place where everything we do is somehow contrived. Our perversions. Our morality. The more I think of questions like this, the more confused I get. So maybe it doesn't pay to think. I think it was Socrates who said that the unexamined life was not worth living. So maybe unreflective action is mere existence, not true living. But when I get reflective, I usually get a headache no pill can end—unless I drug myself to sleep. Even then my dreams tend to be disturbing.

I guess it's time to hit the road again. Head out West again. It is time. My friend and I are running out of tricks to amuse ourselves. What was stimulating yesterday is boring today. Some of the stuff we tried is downright scary. If we miscalculate, one or another of us is going to be really hurt. No fun anymore. Can't finish the 120 days of Sodom. At least I can't. I think one or the other of us would be dead by day 45.

JANUARY 30, 1967

Dear Samuel,

Gallatin, Ohio. Named after Albert Gallatin, Secretary of the Treasury. He lived from 1761–1849. One of the signers of the Treaty of Ghent ending the War of 1812. Trick question. When was the War of 1812 fought? It actually dragged out to 1815—and you already know about the Battle of New Orleans. That war was fought after the actual war was declared to be over. So maybe you never heard of Gallatin. I hadn't. Small, small town. I suppose they teach the schoolchildren how the town got its name. There's a Ghent, Ohio, too. You can learn a lot of history from place names. Or not, as the case may be. They could probably find someone more famous to name the town after, but it's a small town—and they only got a 1-1/4 cent stamp to commemorate. What does one do with a 1-1/4 cent stamp? How do you pay for it? I'd like a 1-1/4 cent stamp please. That will be 1-1/4 cents. Here's a 8-1/2 cent coin. Good. I owe you 7-1/4 cents in change.

March 15, 1967

Dear Samuel,

I'm traveling around the heartland, as it were. I did get to Tennessee. OK, a bit of a border state. The stamp honors Old Hickory—Andrew Jackson—in the Prominent American Series. Military hero, Seventh President of the U.S. He gets a ten-cent stamp—not 1-1/4 cents. I guess there is some relationship between fame and the denomination of the stamp—sometimes. Is Washington only worth a one-dollar and Jackson a twenty-dollar bill? Lincoln only five? Who knows? I am headed back East. I don't trust myself in the South yet. Even in a border state. I don't trust myself at all.

March 17, 1967

Dear Samuel,

Mad drive to get to NYC in two days. Why do I bother? You can get all those first-day covers from your dealer. I suppose that's not much fun. This way you get a letter from me to spice up your life. I don't know how much spice my words add to the meat and potatoes of your life. Maybe you get spice from other sources and don't need any more from me. But I'm playing the game as best I can. A bit of an adrenaline rush. Can I speed through one state after another without getting pulled over by a cop and ticketed or even worse? Two days from Hermitage, Tennessee, to NYC in time for the new UN stamp. Several new issues. The new headquarters of the UN Development Programme (again, notice the spelling) and the Children's Fund. Celebration of new nations—the ones pictured are Lesotho and Rwanda. The colonial empires are finally giving up control of their colonies—more or less willingly. Who knows what the future holds for these fledglings? A few educated or powerful rulers—masses of people, underfed, underemployed—with loyalty to families, clans, and tribes rather than to nations made up of all different and frequently warring tribes. In the U.S. the movement toward independence was led by a minority of what the British would call radical hotheads. They used the same language to describe the leaders of the liberation movements in India and Africa. But we initially had a large number of highly educated people to lead us. And look at the problems we had to cope with—including a really bloody Civil War 85 years after the country was founded. And still today, riots in Watts. We're still not there. And the leaders of the down-trodden—Adam Clayton Powell ousted from the House of Representatives for misuse of public funds. Was he targeted because he has a big mouth and doesn't pull his punches when he talks about racial matters, or did he betray a public trust and deserve what he got? If you're going to be a gadfly, you've got to expect that people will try to swat you. And you shouldn't be handing them a fly swatter and then complain when they connect and leave you lying in the dust. At the same time, I wonder if we ousted every Representative for misuse of public funds, would we have enough honest people left to make up a quorum? And if this is business as usual here, how much more so in countries like Rwanda and Lesotho? Maybe education is not enough. If you have a highly educated, intelligent, crooked, corrupt, or biased people, maybe all you have done is to produce more clever crooks. I'm not one to believe in the myth of the noble savage. People tout the virtues of our native American population. OK, we treated them poorly—herded them into reservations on the poorest land we could find, massacred them when they resisted, stole their children and brainwashed them in missionary schools, broke treaty after treaty with them, treated them like savages (them or us?). But there were Indian wars before the Europeans got here. I don't think the different tribes treated each other too kindly. I think some of them kidnapped enemy women and children and used them like slaves. What can we expect of Africans only a few years past bush country? The representatives look fine enough dressed either in formal European or African attire. They speak well. But that doesn't mean that people back home are ready to be—I hate to use the word *civilized* (are we?). And in the General Assembly, each one of these dots on a world map gets the same vote as Australia and Germany—and the good old USA. Should make for some interesting debates on the floor of the General Assembly.

March 30, 1967

Dear Samuel,

One hundredth anniversary of the Alaska Purchase. The envelope shows William H. Seward and the Russian Ambassador at the time. The purchase was marked at the time as Seward's Folly. All that barren land—even for two cents an acre. I'm sure the Russians regret having sold it. All that gold soon to be discovered. A large foothold in the New World. I can't get to Sitka. A bit too much of a trek, considering the time. You'll get that one from your dealer. I wouldn't mind going to Alaska someday. The last frontier. Climb up a 21,000-foot mountain. Hobnob with the moose and the grizzly bears—even with polar bears. You lose your sense of perspective in NYC. You get to think the whole world operates that way. There are more people in Brooklyn than in the whole state of Alaska. It might be nice to go trekking for days at a time—not to see any people at all, just animals, to live off the land. Fish for food. It might be nice. Someday.

April 28, 1967

Dear Samuel,

Still in NYC. Big happenings. Martin Luther King led a big anti-war parade in the city. He's trying to show that he's not a one-issue person—that Blacks can have more on their mind than just Black issues. They can have an American agenda every bit as complex as a white person. Not every Black leader agrees with him. The radicals think he's diluting his message. The moderates don't want whites to write him off because of his stand against the war. Sometimes the true leaders have to take an unpopular stand to maintain their principles. Even if you disagree with his stand, you can admire him for having the courage to take it. I wouldn't mind having a leader like that in the Governor's mansion. It might tempt me to return.

OK, the stamps. A bit unusual, 4 stamps actually—Peace, Justice, Fraternity, and Truth. I'm not sure where Fraternity fits in. Maybe the French influence. Liberté, Egalité, Fraternité. No Truth. Back then everything had to come in threes. Life, Liberty, and the Pursuit of Happiness. I guess if Newton could boil down all the laws of physics into three statements—all the laws of planetary motion—we should be able to do the same for government and society. But all that without Truth. Not much Truth kicking around these days.

Fraternité—does that include the women? I include women. My friend. The freedom to experiment with another person as an equal. I'm not sure where Truth comes into any of what we do together. It's getting . . . scary.

MAY 25, 1967

Dear Samuel,

I'm in Canada. Really. The first time I've been outside the U.S. The World's Fair. The U.S. Pavilion. The stamp celebrates the centennial of the Canadian Federation. It shows the fathers of the Confederation. Fathers, not mothers. I'm not sure how strong the Federation is these days. The French in Quebec are flexing their muscles. They want the language of the province to be French—Canadian French. No bilingualism. They're talking about separating from the Confederation. Sound familiar? Only the issue here isn't slavery or segregation. Would the Federal government go to war to keep Quebec in the Confederation? Interesting prospect. What would the U.S. stand be in such a conflict? Probably with the Union. If every country split up over questions of language and ethnicity, we wouldn't have a viable government anywhere in the world. Just a bunch of mini-countries squabbling about past grievances.

The Viet Nam war drags on. The heavyweight champion of the boxing world gets stripped of his crown because he won't join the Army and fight for the U.S., right or wrong. Worse, he calls himself a Moslem now and says that as a Moslem he has no cause to fight against other men of color. Interesting. Blacks becoming Moslems. They don't seem to know anything about the Arab slave trade in Africa. Just what the Europeans did. Europeans did enough evil. The Arabs weren't much better. Maybe even worse. I guess when you look at history, you have to make choices, even if they wind up making little sense. My choice. Take a breather. Leave NYC on two feet before they carry me off in a box. Carry me where? Where do I want my bones to lie for all eternity? Do I even care?

June 19, 1967

Dear Samuel,

Back in NYC. Why? Not for the stamps alone. The UN celebrates the Year of the Tourist. Leave home and see the world. I don't need any encouragement. I am seeing the world—at least the U.S. part of it. Like a tourist. An eternal tourist looking for a place—to rest.

The Supreme Court ruled unanimously that all laws against inter-racial marriage are illegal. Unconstitutional. That should go over big in the South. Do you want your sister marrying one of . . . THEM? If I had a sister. If she really wanted to. I met an inter-racial couple around here. Neither set of parents were enchanted by the match. I said I couldn't understand why—since both of them were Methodists. Sure.

And now the Supreme Court has its first Black Justice. I can hear my father ranting and raving about it. What kind of justice can you expect from a court with niggers handing down the opinions. Nigger justice. Had that back in Reconstruction. We took care of the carpetbaggers, the scalawags, and the niggers back then. We can do it again. My father talks big. He can light up the night with burning crosses. He can act pretty bravely hiding behind a mask with a bunch of his cronies beside him. I'll tell you, if I would want to marry someone of another race, I wouldn't do it in Alabama, in spite of what the Supreme Court has said. Some of them are not known as liberals. Some of them must be Southern. I guess at some point, law trumps sentiment—at least in the Supreme Court. Main Street is another matter. I'm still playing footsy with my friend. I'm amazed I'm still here.

JULY 4, 1967

Dear Samuel,

Rome, NY. The 150th anniversary of the Erie Canal connecting Albany and Buffalo. Way back then they moved barges along with mules. The envelope features one of the many songs that celebrated the Canal—fifteen years on the Erie Canal. How about a canal between NYC and Birmingham and Atlanta? Interesting. You can write to me about it if anything happens.

JULY 5, 1967

Dear Samuel,

Chicago. I'm trying to stay out of NYC for a while. Chicago is nice. Sold some toys to an adult store—books, magazines, movies, and such. The owner got to talking about the trade. He told me that to make a profit, a book has to sell at least 23,000 copies. He showed me a paperback with a clearly homosexual title, but the cover shows a peeping tom looking at a scantily clad buxom blonde. The book targeted men who were tired of heterosexual porn but still got turned on by heterosexual visual images. There must be at least 23,000 men with that peculiar taste. Imagine. And the nudist magazines—very specialized. Some only show frontal nudity in the women. Some included older people with less than ideal figures. Some included children. Each type of magazine has its own audience. I won't even begin to tell you about the special audiences for S and M. You add all this up, and there is a huge market for porn. You would never know it to hear some people speak. But behind closed doors. I guess I hit upon a lucrative field. It is getting more lucrative every day. The feminists are all talking about a woman's right to a fulfilling sex life. What they call fulfilling would not have been imagined 30 years ago. Let them talk. They are my best advertising.

The stamp honors the 50th anniversary of the Lions International—serving the blind with guide dogs and searching for peace. I suppose they do some good work while they are socializing. I was never one for socializing in such groups. Secret hand signals, insignias, etc. Then again in all my wanderings, I haven't helped a single blind person to get across the street. Maybe I should join a society of Jackals International—to teach members how to survive in a hostile environment using your wits alone. I haven't been doing so badly, all things considered. Part of my background as a child between my father, whom I wished wasn't there, and my mother, who really wasn't there. Not bad, if I say so myself. A triumph of a really resourceful child in the face of adversity. Yeah, team!

July 12, 1967

Dear Samuel,

Back East, but not in NY. The stamp commemorates the birth of Thoreau 150 years ago. American poet (I never read his poetry), naturalist, and author of, among other things, *Walden*. I've read that book many times. He was trying to lead a simple life. Pay attention to the natural surroundings. Don't move too fast through the world, chasing materialistic dreams. I had a deep feeling for that idea once. There were four or five of us on a circular trail. They left me behind, looking at a single spider reacting to the bugs that flew into her web. I could have stayed there for hours. When the others returned, they told me about the things they saw that I had missed. I could have told them what I had seen that they had missed. You can either go out into the world and watch things stream by or sit still and watch things stream by. Maybe next year I'll figure it all out. Meanwhile the wanderlust has hit me again. I'll stop from time to time. By and by. Buy and buy. Bye.

July 29, 1967

Dear Samuel,

It's started again in earnest. Firebombing the home of a Civil Rights worker in Mobile. Mobile, not Birmingham. Riots in Detroit. Dozens killed. Forty-seven hundred Federal troops sent to quell the riots. The looting. Homes destroyed. Lives. The President sets up an advisory committee on civil disorders to figure out the causes. He designates tomorrow as a national day of prayer for reconciliation. Tell that to the bombers in Mobile. The monster has escaped from his cage. Two monsters—one roaming the countryside. People pretending it isn't even there. Or smiling smugly, because it only attacks certain houses. Certain people. Them. The ones that live on the other side of the tracks. And now a second monster. Slouching toward Jerusalem.

I am safely in Nebraska—in Lincoln. Where is Lincoln now that we need him? Nebraska is 100 years old today. Another border state. The stamp has a cow on it. Maybe a steer. Bum steer. Corn. Hooch. The first Governor was David Butler. Good to know if you're ever on a quiz program. Big quiz now. Name the dead in Detroit. Name the person whose home was bombed in Mobile. Le Flore. The flower. Flowers don't do well in fire. People, too, can burn.

I have to leave Lincoln. People are beginning to recognize who I am. The part that accepts punishment. Only that part. They are willing to accommodate that part. To punish me. The anger in me is bottled up inside me. Growing. I have dreams of setting fires. Vivid. In Chicago. Working with O'Leary's cow. Watching the whole city burn. I don't want to do a thing. Detroit is already burning without me. I don't have to do a thing.

August 1, 1967

Dear Samuel,

Back in DC. That was quick. I drove straight through. Caught a few hours of sleep by the side of the road. Barely ate anything. The stamp celebrates the International Broadcasting System of the U.S. Information Agency—the Voice of America. They have their job cut out for them. The cradle of democracy is burning. Racism is alive and well. Bird coming home to rest. Not to rest. To rip and tear. To maim. How does that read in Paris? In Rome? In Moscow? Ah . . . I told you so. Hypocrisy. Make the world safe for democracy. Clean up the world, while your own home reeks of filth and stench.

They are finding me here in DC. It begins innocently enough. Polite conversation at a bar. It moves on from there. My place or yours? It moves quickly to . . . my quirk or yours? And the quirk is always S and M. S for them and M for me. Unrestrained. Bondage and more whips and chains. The last two women, Black as coal. Couldn't get you in Detroit. Too far away. How about here in DC? Where could I go from here? Find a place to heal. Not heel. I am tired of that. Dog tired.

October 2, 1967

Dear Samuel,

DC. I didn't get away. Somehow . . . I couldn't. This city of classic buildings. Neoclassical buildings. City of monuments and statues. Site of the celebration of the 50th anniversary of the American institute of Urban Planners Meeting to discuss the rehabilitation of American cities. That's good. The stamp celebrates planning for better cities. As if putting up the right kind of buildings would eliminate the problems. Down South it was easy. Put us on one side of the tracks and them on the other. You always knew where you were. One side had sidewalks and streetlamps. The other side didn't. And you had better know which side to be on once the evening sun went down.

Neoclassic buildings? Like a Roman city. But Rome fell. What was going on in those buildings once the sun went down? I can tell you what goes on here. Decadence. Debauchery. Everybody's doing it. Senators. Representatives. Me. I can't get away from it. They search me out. Ripped and torn. I have to get away. Somewhere.

October 6, 1967

Dear Samuel,

Finland, Minnesota. Did you know such a place existed? Tiny town. In the middle of noplace. The stamp celebrates the 50th anniversary of Finnish independence. Independence from whom? I'll have to look that one up. My knowledge of Finnish history is surprisingly meager. I'll bet they do a good job of teaching that in the schools here. Let us celebrate, class. Marshall Mannerheim, supreme champion of liberty. He helped forge a new constitution and stabilize the government. He was the commander of the Army. Oh, Generalimisso Mannerheim. Welcome to the USA. Would you help us with our constitution. Help us stabilize our government. Finish the job we couldn't do for ourselves. It's only been 191 years. Give us time. Just a little more time. We have a Black man now in the Supreme Court. See. The process is working. A southern jury convicted 7 of 18 accused killers of Civil Rights workers in Mississippi. That's more than a third. See. The Heat of the Night. The Great White Hope. We are beginning to face our past now. Putting it on the big screen so everybody can watch—in vivid color, not just Black and White. Maybe we can do it on our own. Besides, Mr. Mannerheim, he dead. Looked at his heart of darkness and just collapsed on the spot. Kill the bloody savages. In Helsinki. In Finland, Minnesota. Don't see any savages. Check the mirror. They are just ourselves.

OCTOBER 24, 1967

Dear Samuel,

NYC. I took a circuitous route to get here. Do I really want to be here?

UN stamp. Toward Disarmament—they shall beat their swords into plowshares. One stamp in English, one is French. Why French? Why not Spanish or Russian or Chinese? Toward disarmament—elsewhere. People stockpiling arms here, waiting for the next lynching. The next riots. Could be here. Again. Death at an early age. The Destruction of the hearts and minds of Negro schoolchildren in the Boston Public schools. Boston. Not Birmingham. Let him who is without sin cast the first stone. Why accuse Boston? Glass houses. Don't throw stones anymore. Molotov cocktails. Who was Molotov anyway? Nice to be remembered. What's in a name? Could just as easily be a Connor cocktail or a Stokely Carmichael cocktail. Don't ask for whom the bell tolls. It tolls for thee.

NOVEMBER 2, 1967

Dear Samuel,

DC. The stamp shows a picture of a painting. Nice colors. Thomas Eakins, 1844–1916. So . . . fiftieth anniversary of his death. When did they start commemorating the death, not the birth? Is there a hidden message here? Eakins. Famous American artist. Painter of portraits and sporting scenes. I remember one of his paintings of boxers going at it in the ring. Pretty grim. That's it. Art. Can be beautiful even when grim. Poetry as well. Baudelaire. I remember. Beautiful poetry about the rotting corpse of an old whore under a tree. About a sex crime. Decapitation. A woman. I am getting there. The decapitatee, not the decapitator. Eakins. Dissection scene at a medical school. Blood and guts rendered so realistically, you could probably figure out the cause of death. The body. Donated to science. Let people cut me in death as they did in life. Look at these scars. These internal injuries. Is that consistent with any disease you're aware of? Class. Come on. There is a disease of the soul. Probably hereditary. Consult Krafft-Ebing. What page? You'll have to find out for yourselves. The 33rd edition. It's in the library. Indexed for your convenience. While you're looking, I'll be out on the Delaware in my racing scull. Along with the Biglin brothers. They were famous once. And now they're dead. Being dissected in some medical school. From scull to school. From cutting through the water to being cut up and then simply thrown away. Discarded. What's the difference? Dead is dead. A tomb. A garbage heap. It all comes to the same thing. People die so that flies can live. I of all people should know that. I of all people. Aye.

November 17, 1967

Dear Samuel,

NYC. Nice stamp. First Eakins, now Chagall. Glass windows. Stained glass. In honor of Dag Hammerskjold and those that died with him when his plane went down. Russian Jewish painter honoring a Scandinavian diplomat. Black Mayor elected in Cleveland and in Gary, Indiana. We may get out of this yet. In one peace.

December 11, 1967

Dear Samuel,

The year draws to a close. I stayed in NYC. Not in Natchez to celebrate the 150th anniversary of Mississippi statehood. To remember its first Governor—David Holmes. You remember him? Probably had to remember the names of all the Governors of all the Southern states. Got to see a showing of the movie *Guess Who's Coming to Dinner*. I bet that will play well in Birmingham. Got to see the movie with my friend. Will I make it to the end of the year?

January 24, 1968

Dear Samuel,

DC. American flag. Envelope shows building of first White House in 1788 that the British burned in 1812. The best-laid plans of mice and men often go awry. Between the conception and the reality falls the shadow. Man plans. God laughs. My life. Having a hard time keeping it together. Keeping my spirits up. That's a good term for it. Spirits. Strong spirits. But the flesh is weak.

JANUARY 29, 1968

Dear Samuel,

Philadelphia. I haven't been here for a while. Celebrate Thomas Paine. Prominent American Series. Championed the cause of independence during the Revolutionary War. These are the times that try men's souls. Wrote Common Sense, something to think about. Is common sense all that common? All these rationalists 200 years ago. Faith that all reasonable men, if given the facts, would come up with the same conclusions. They didn't. Of course. America's great patriot was England's rabble rouser. Were they less educated? Less reasonable?

The President sends Congress a message urging the passage of Civil Rights legislation. Do you see any common sense here? Men of equal intellect coming to an inevitable conclusion. I remember reading how the Founding Fathers justified forming a republic in such a large nation with so many conflicting viewpoints and religious convictions and regional concerns. They said all the factions would balance each other out so that one faction couldn't take total control. Isn't this a recognition that there is no common sense we can appeal to? Just eternal conflict. Compromise by necessity, not by conviction. Isn't that where we are now? A point of compromise, because otherwise we will wind up ripping ourselves apart. Pragmatism, not principle. But sometimes in the heat of battle, even pragmatism gets lost.

FEBRUARY 12, 1968

Dear Samuel,

Shawneetown, Illinois. Land of Lincoln. Tiny town in the Southwest corner near the border with Kentucky. Why here? Who knows? A dot on the map. One dot or another. 150 years of statehood. You wouldn't think that Illinois came into the Union after Louisiana and Mississippi.

The envelope shows the old statehouse in Vandalia (Illinois, not Mississippi), where Lincoln served as a Legislator—and Bryant cottage in Bement, where Lincoln and Douglas prepared for their debates. I'll have to go back and read the debates—which put Lincoln on the political map.

Obscure towns. Seemingly small events that get magnified over time. Become significant. Students protesting in South Carolina. Orangeburg. You could expect arrests. Beatings. Not shooting. Killing. A hundred years from now, that is all the town will be known for. Everything else will pale by comparison. Oh yes. You're from Orangeburg. That's where the students were shot down. Murdered. Oh. I had nothing to do with that. All I know is what I read in the papers. And you didn't hear the shots being fired? You didn't see the students falling? Where were you on February 8? I was shopping. I was doing my laundry. I was tending my garden. It was one of your sons that did the shooting. One of your sons that was killed. Look at the newsreels. Look at them over and over again. Look. See, Dick. See, Jane. See their dog, Spot. Run, Spot, run. See Spot run. He is running to that place. He is licking up the blood. Look, Dick. Look, Jane. Spot is licking up the blood. Spot likes to lap up blood. Blood is healthy for dogs. Maybe tomorrow he will drink your blood too.

MARCH 8, 1968

Dear Samuel,

Back in DC. Another prominent American—Oliver Wendell Holmes, 1841–1935. Justice of the Supreme Court. Montgomery ordered to end its dual education system. It's still the Feds taking all the initiative at least on that side of the fence. When will the locals figure out what has to be done and not to merely resist and then comply? Figure out what is in their best interest—like when Birmingham figured out how to get rid of Bull Connor. We have insight. We have intelligence. Initiative. Why do we let ourselves be led by Yahoos and cheer them on? No cheering from this neck of the woods. But I'm too far away. Too . . . preoccupied.

MARCH 15, 1968

Dear Samuel,

Fiftieth anniversary of the American Legion. God and Country. Veterans are citizens. Their headquarters are in Indianapolis. Why is the stamp not issued there? OK, I was never much impressed with Indianapolis. I once asked several people on the street what was there to do in town. One person said that there was little or nothing to do since they closed down the burlesque shows. Another told me I was a little late. The one movie theater that showed foreign and independent films burned down. Most people in town thought it was an act of God. I read the newspaper. The *Star*. The editorial page was somewhat to the right of Attila the Hun. Indiana is like three states. The South feels like Alabama or Mississippi. The central part is farm country. Farmers for the most part are politically conservative by nature. The north part is dominated by east-European immigrants working in heavy industry. They remember the Blacks that came up from the South and were used as scab labor to break the backs of the Unions. No love lost there. So I guess the *Star* serves the needs of the State. If you want liberal or moderate views, you have to get the Indiana edition of the *Louisville Courier*. That was my impression of Indiana. Maybe that's why the American Legion chose Indianapolis for its home city. They feel right at home there. So I'm still in DC, not in Indianapolis. I have the feeling I have to hit the road again.

JUNE 15, 1968

Dear Samuel,

NYC. It's been almost three months since my last letter. Three months. Like an age. As if time stood still. News initially promising. A Black named Assistant Superintendent of the Jefferson County Schools. A Black as a serious contender in Roosevelt City. A black elected to the Roosevelt City Council. Small steps towards something like normalcy. I shouldn't have gotten my hopes up. The news of King's assassination in Memphis. I think King anticipated the possibility. You stick your neck out, and somebody is going to get pissed. Maybe a whole lot of somebodies getting together and setting someone up to do the job. But it doesn't matter. Somebody. Somebodies. One body. And then it got interesting. One week later, the signing of the Civil Rights Act. The Fair Housing Act banning discrimination in the sale or rental of housing. It's as if King purchased this act with his blood. What a price to pay for what should have been done years ago. Because it was right. Not as a gesture too late for King to appreciate. Ah, you say. King is looking down from the Heavens and smiling. I would rather see him smiling here on earth. He had a lot more work to accomplish. What now? Who can fill his shoes?

Well, there are others. Maybe not quite as dynamic. I think the forces that wanted King out of the way are going to be disappointed when others put on the mantle of leadership. Abernathy led the poor people's march in DC. He's not quite the speaker King was, but the crowds came anyway. It must be really disturbing to the Yahoos to see that the march included poor people of all shades and colors. It's not just a Black thing anymore. If the Movement forms an alliance between poor Whites and poor Blacks, the powers that be can't pit them against each other anymore. The poor white trash and the field niggers together would make a powerful force for change. Maybe that's why they had King killed. He was in Memphis to support garbage workers of any race. He was forming an alliance with Chicano fruit pickers in California. That starts to get really scary in some circles.

The Justice Department rejected the segregated school system in the South. The so-called Freedom of Choice initiative. You let poor White and Black children discover that they're all just children. That's real trouble.

Real trouble. Riots all over the U.S. Riots in DC. Futile to appeal to the rioters that King preached non-violence. Look at where it got him. Riots in 125 cities—Baltimore, Chicago, Kansas City. You can't take anything for granted anywhere. I don't know where all this will end. I used to feel safe in some cities. Not anymore. I see young Blacks, and I cower. Call it one manifestation of Black Power. Call it what you will.

I stick around DC just to be close to what is going on in the capital. All the news as it happens. And there was a woman. Another woman. I'll tell you a secret. I think she has a touch of Black in her. We haven't talked about that. It kind of heightens the S and M business. To think I might be putting myself at the mercy of someone who—how shall I say it—who felt the pain more strongly. I felt such a mixture of helplessness and anger when I heard the news. When the Poor People's march came to DC, I was there. I didn't quite join the marchers. I didn't think I deserved to march with them. I stood along the route—with her. I kept looking at her to see how she was reacting. We never talked about it. But after, her behavior toward me was more resolute. I still bear some marks on me. They join the others.

She tried to get me to be the aggressor in turns. I couldn't do it. She demanded it of me. I tried. Maybe if I thought she was pure White, if there is such a thing anymore. It has become an issue between us. She walked out on me. She was furious. I went bar hopping afterward, trying to find someone to take her place. Anyone. No luck. I don't want someone to just go through the motions. To pretend. I want someone to really do it. To find it . . . satisfying.

I ran back to NYC. Maybe I could find my friend again. If she could keep things a bit restrained. I am not getting any younger. My body is not as resilient as it used to be.

I got the most recent stamp. Fiftieth anniversary of the International Labor Organization, headquartered in Geneva. I can't think of anything to say about it. Can't think of much to say about anything. I seem to be all played out. I'm just going through the paces.

JUNE 27, 1968

Dear Samuel,

So why am I back in DC again so soon? I felt like a caged animal in NY. OK, it was a big cage. But I found myself pacing back and forth with no sense of purpose or direction. OK. I restocked. Even sold a few things. A person has to eat. Then I thought, maybe I should stay out on the street and hustle for food. I felt like I was on the third floor of a building and had to go down to the basement. Down among the rats and roaches, where I belonged. I didn't. Not yet. I suppose if I wanted to, I could probably find a cellar here as well.

I got you the current stamp. An eagle on a weather vane exhorting people to register to vote. The image on the envelope was an election in 1840. All white males wearing ties and jackets and top hats—putting their ballots in a box. No women, of course. No blacks. Are they trying to tell us subtly that times have changed? You can vote in jeans if you like. Even if you're poor or female or Black. So do it. I can't. I'm registered to vote in Birmingham. I'm not in Birmingham anymore. I guess you could say I'm not a good citizen. But the price is still too high for my return. Maybe somewhere down the line.

JULY 4, 1968

Dear Samuel,

July 4. Independence Day. I suppose I should celebrate. Here I am in Pittsburgh. The Birmingham of the North, as it were. Smog City until steel began to decline and they decided to clear the air. The city looks a bit like Birmingham. A lot of hills. A lot of trees. I tried to imagine what it would be like to be home. July. It would be hot. It's pretty hot here as well.

Pretty stamps. Historical. The flags of the colonists before the nation became a nation. Before the Betsy Ross flag became official. One flag after—with 15 stars. Interesting idea. A way of getting collectors to buy 9 or 10 stamps instead of just one. There is Washington's Cruiser flag, the Bunker Hill flag, the Bennington flag, the Rhode Island flag, the Fort McHenry flag—the one that inspired Francis Scott Key to write the Star-Spangled Banner—the Grand Union flag, the Fort Moultrie flag, and the Philadelphia Lighthouse flag. The one I missed was the one with the rattlesnake on it that said, "Don't tread on me."

I went to an open-air exhibit. Nice. Some degree of culture in this town. I stopped by a statue of a woman—life-sized. She is heavy with child. Substantial arms and legs, but a graceful neck and a jaunty look on her face as she stares off into space. The statue was entitled *Pregnancy Is a State of Mind*. It was a nice statue. But I found it more rewarding to hear the comments of the people when they looked at the statue and then read the title. Most of the comments by women. A lot of women. I started fantasizing. I had to restrain myself. It's getting harder all the time. You can't just go up to a stranger and ask her to beat on you. Lacerate your flesh. My flesh. Oh, that this all too sordid flesh might melt. Sordid. Solid. Stolid. Would you? Please. Don't bother me, or I'll call a cop. Stop. Skip to my loo. P. U. I'll be leaving Pittsburgh before they run me in. Incarcerate. Phlebotimate. I can't wait.

August 1, 1968

Dear Samuel,

Page, Arizona. Out West again. Wide open places. The stamp honors John Wesley Powell, 1834–1902—geologist, ethnologist, explorer—on the 100th anniversary of his trip down the Colorado River in something like a rowboat. Amazing. Intrepid. Worthy of recognition. Perdition. Fruition. Delusion.

What makes a man head down a river into the unknown—a really wild river. Symbolic. Life. A wild river. Some boats get overturned. Upended. Suspended. Not me. I want safe passage. I portage past the white water. Carry my boat along the river. Strange sight. A boat being carried over the rocks—not carrying over the water. Carry me home. Swing low, sweet chariot. Michael rowed the boat. Ashore. Jordan River is deep and wide. Meet my mother on the other side. Meet my mother. What would she look like? I don't know. I wouldn't even recognize her. No photos. Not one. Not one.

September 20, 1968

Dear Samuel,

Sault Sainte Marie, Michigan. The 300th anniversary of the exploration of Jacques Marquette through the Wisconsin, Mississippi, and Illinois Rivers in a canoe. Not so dangerous. But lonely. Probably more dangers from other men than from animals. But lonely. I wandered lonely as a cloud. I wandered. What am I looking for? What was Marquette looking for? The unknown. To make the unknown known. And then the settlers moved in.

I stopped at a bar for a beer. The TV was on. News program. Black actress. She is not a maid. She is a star in her own right. Millions watch. Amazing. A Black woman who is not a maid. Who doesn't say Yes'm. Is she a nurse—a doctor even? Does she know about birthing babies? She combs her hair neatly. Dresses discreetly. Quotes from Phyllis Wheatley. The world is changing. The program will be seen in Michigan. In Mississippi, Georgia, and Alabama. By people like my father. What will he say? The black bitch looks really fine. Drinks French wine. I wonder. Would she be a connoisseur of S and M? I fantasize. More and more. Silks. Satins. Gore. More. I beg. I implore. She smiles coyly. Bares her teeth. Growls. Roars. I know what is in store. I ask for more. I am shaken to the core. Stricken. I don't think I will last through the night. I take flight. My plight. No fight left. I left that war . . . all right.

October 1, 1968

Dear Samuel,

Little Rock, Arkansas. I sneak in unnoticed. The Arkansas Navigation Project—from the Mississippi River to Catoosa, Oklahoma. Hydroelectric Power. Flood Control. Bank Stabilization. Water Supply. Recreation. Man trying to control Nature. It never quite works according to plan. A man. An artificial waterway. Nature always finds a way to get even. You try to control people. People get even. It may take a while. The best-laid plans of mice and men. I feel uneasy here. The image of young schoolchildren. Jeering mobs of white people. Ordinary people. Churchgoing people shouting obscenities. Federal troops. I don't want to be here. I don't want to be here anymore.

OCTOBER 15, 1968

Dear Samuel,

Ponca City, Oklahoma. Due North of Oklahoma City—just South of the border with Kansas. On U.S. route 177, if that helps any. The stamp commemorates the Dramatic Land Rush of 1893—175,000 people set out in covered wagons to stake out homesteads in Oklahoma, the Northwest section. Why? Why commemorate it in 1968? OK, the 175th anniversary. That makes sense. They called it the Cherokee Strip. That makes less sense. Did they displace the Cherokees to make room for white settlers? And why the other migration—the forced migration? The Trail of Tears. The Cherokee didn't originate here. They came from Tennessee. In the middle of winter. On foot. More than half of them died en route. From the fertile lands of Tennessee to the most barren region the government could find. And then the irony. They discovered oil on the land. What to do then? Move the Injuns out. Promise them something and then take it back. When I was a child, we talked about Indian givers. People who gave and then took back. I always thought it was the Indian they were talking about—not the white man who gave to the Indians. Give, then take away again. Why not a stamp to commemorate the Trail of Tears? Oh, sorry. We need to honor the doctrine of Manifest Destiny. God put the Indians there to test our resolve. Our courage to overcome obstacles. Over their dead bodies. Wherever I go, there is an odor of death. We honor the Conquerors, not the victims. History is written by the winners. Have you ever read a history of the U.S. written by an Indian? What would he say about the opening of the Cherokee Strip? Would we give his book to schoolchildren to read? Required reading? Test on the material next Tuesday. These are the times that try men's souls. But we fail miserably. We fail miserably.

Back in NYC. The play *The Great White Hope* opens. All about a Black boxer and a White boxer. The Whites all hoping that the White man would win—especially since the Black man was uppity. He had the nerve to associate with white women. This one fight was supposed to prove the superiority of the White race. They did it again when Joe Louis was champion. Hitler tried to do it in the 1936 Olympic games. He couldn't stand the idea that a Black man could beat his Aryan athletes in track and field. Well, they could. Hitler blocked some German athletes from competing because they were Jewish. Can't let reality triumph over ideology. Blacks are in the Major Leagues now. No one gives it a second thought. They did, though, when Jackie Robinson first played for the Dodgers. Yesterday's unthinkable becomes today's routine. Maybe that's the hope. People will get tired of hating and just settle down to the business of living. Live and let live. So why then is the play running to sold-out audiences? Why bring the painful past up again? To rub salt in old wounds? Allow us to congratulate ourselves for getting past that point of narrow-mindedness—and into another place that we're hardly aware of. Marcel Marceau again. Moving from one glass cell to another. Invisible. But with walls as strong as steel.

November 1, 1968

Dear Samuel,

I am back East again. DC. The annual Christmas stamp. The religious one, which means the Christian one (why would they have a Jewish or a Hindu Christmas stamp?). Why a religious stamp at all? Are we, in fact, a Christian nation or a nation of people of all faiths? The stamp is based on a painting by Jan Van Eyck that hangs in the National Gallery of Art. Convenient. The Annunciation. Except if you look closely, the picture is not the Madonna but the angel. Is there a hidden message here? There are hidden messages everywhere. Maybe the name of the painter. I don't know. The Annunciation. On the Christian calendar, that took place on August 15. I'm not much of a Christian. I was never drilled in catechism. I might be missing all kinds of clues. You ever look closely at a dollar bill. Try to figure out the imagery—a pyramid with a human eye on top. All kinds of clues. People sending secret messages in secret codes. They pass right by unnoticed. Van Eyck. He was Dutch. New York was once a Dutch settlement. Is there a connection here? Damned if I know. Maybe damned if I don't.

NOVEMBER 22, 1968

Dear Samuel,

NYC. I'm here—250,000 marching in DC for jobs and freedom only a few days after I left. I never seem to be where the action is.

Big controversy after the Summer games. Tommie Smith and John Carlos after winning medals in racing raise their fists in a Black Power gesture. Some want to strip them of their medals. The Olympics are supposed to be just about athletes, not politics. Well . . . not quite. Witness Hitler in 1936. The rivalries between the USSR and Czechoslovakia, between the USSR and the USA. Tell me there's no politics involved. The banning of South Africa from the games because of their apartheid policies. So two athletes held up their fists protesting their country's racial policies. After all that has been happening around the country, it was bound to happen sooner or later. If the Games are purely about athleticism and those two ran faster than anybody else, then they deserve their medals. You don't have to like a person to acknowledge his ability. Remember Ty Cobb? The Georgia Peach. Great player. In the Hall of Fame. Miserable human being. Spiked opposing players when he slid into a base. Consciously. I wouldn't want to associate with the man. But he was a great player nonetheless.

The plane on the stamp is supposed to be flying over Madison Square Garden. Maybe during a heavyweight championship fight. Was Rocky Marciano kind to dogs? Was Sonny Liston a good husband?

The UN issues a stamp today as well. International Year for Human Rights. Are we any closer to realizing that goal anywhere in the world? Is this just wishful thinking? Is mankind prone eternally to deprive his fellow human beings of the most basic rights? I can't let myself get too cynical. I have met truly magnanimous people in my travels. I have read about any number of people who could qualify as saints. It's just that their efforts are dwarfed by the magnitude of evil of a Hitler or a Stalin. Has it always been this way? Will it always be this way?

DECEMBER 3, 1968

Dear Samuel,

Boston. Another year almost gone. It has been . . . very trying. The Post Office seems to like to end the year focusing on art—this time on William M. Harnett. I will admit to you that I didn't know his work before. Famous American artist. I guess I'm not up on the whole range of American artists. A painter of still life—what the French would call La Nature Morte, dead nature. Not much nature in the picture—some ancient instruments, a pitcher, a sheet of an old manuscript. When the Dutch painted like this back in the 17th century, not only did they demonstrate their great artistic technique, but they were trying to send a message as well—mostly a moral or religious message. Memento mori. Remember that you will die. Flowers wilt. Fruits rot. The human face gets reduced to a skull. A bit sardonic. But the picture is pleasant enough. The technique esthetic. And if so, maybe the subject matter doesn't matter. You may go out of your way to paint gloomily or preserve subjects just to demonstrate the positive nature of the art itself. Like Baudelaire writing about a sex murder. No art can be purely nihilistic. The picture is an assertion of the value of the effort to create it.

Some things to note at the end of the year. A black woman has been elected to Congress. Private colleges funded by public money are now subject to Civil Rights laws. That's a big one. From the Federal Court. Of course.

Big to-do on TV. An interracial kiss in an episode of *Star Trek*. Wow! Where do we go from here? To recognize that black and white couples have been doing more than kissing for years—whether it was legally recognized or not. Otherwise where did all those light-skinned Negros come from? People of Color. Blacks. Call them what you will. At least what percentage of the genes do you have to have to label a person White or Black? Will we ever get to the point where that kind of speculation will seem meaningless?

December. The holiday season. I met my friend again. I think the next few weeks will be . . . memorable. Will I ever get to see 1969? Or go out in a blaze of glory.

February 10, 1969

Dear Samuel,

Still in NYC. The start of—the continuation of January 1 seems so arbitrary. Who sticks the beginning of the year in the middle of winter. OK, the Winter Solstice. The days are growing longer. But it makes more sense to start the year in the springtime. That's what they did in the Bible. Somewhere along the way, the Bible gets modified or replaced by Roman stuff, and everybody thinks it can't be any other way. It seems . . . unnatural. Not that I'd want to go back to the Bible for everything—stoning adulterous women and rebellious children. That kind of thing. But people get so excited about being in Times Square on New Year's Eve. Watch the ball drop. And at precisely midnight, Voilà. Everything is changed. Everything renewed. Even that is changed. In the Bible the new day begins when the sun goes down. And it was evening and it was morning of Day One. I don't know if that makes any more sense. The day should begin at sunrise. Of course, the sun rises at a different time every day. Then again, so does the sunset. But here we are in the middle of winter—at midnight. And people are going crazy. After a few hours, they get tired. Go home. Sleep off the booze they've consumed. And the next morning it's a new year. They watch parades on TV, unless they're from Philadelphia or Pasadena—where they can be at their own parade. And then comes the football marathon. Bowl games. Rah, team. Before you know it, the first day of the new year is over. I'm tired of this rigamarole. Sick and tired. My friend senses this in me. Exhaustion. Sheer exhaustion. I don't think I have anything physically wrong with me. Call it fin de siècle. But we're not at the end of the century yet. I won't make it that far. The end of the millennium. That might be interesting. Maybe for someone else. The relationship has changed. All that S and M stuff. I'm not up to it anymore. I just lie there with my head in her lap, and she whispers sweet nothings to me in a high-pitched voice like she was talking to an infant. She runs her fingers through my hair and sings lullabies to me. Feeds me half-chewed food. Sometimes pap. Sometimes juice in a sippy cup so

I won't spill it all over myself. Of late she may even give me a bottle. It feels fine to do that. I wonder what she gets out of it day after day. Maybe I am the child she never had. Only it seems I will never grow into childhood. Adulthood. I am regressing. Slipping slowly back to the womb. A full circle of life. The days pass. I am hardly aware of what day of the week it is. Hardly aware of more than her presence. The sound of her voice. She cuddles me to her breast. I . . . want to suckle at her breast. She realizes that. No milk. And then one day, another woman comes. A big black woman. And she has milk. And I do suckle from her breast. It feels like old times. Very old times. That is the way it was back then. Give the baby to a wet nurse. A big black momma. That's the way it must have been with me. My mother dead. Even if not, would she have suckled me? It wasn't done that way back then. It was enough to give birth. Hand the baby over. In my case, not even a choice. Hand the baby over. That big black breast. So comforting. Then raise the baby in the cabin behind the big house. And when the child thinks he knows who he is, yank him out of the cabin, put him back in the big house, and tell him he is the new master of the universe.

Watch the master of the universe suckle. Watch him burp. And then it's time to change his diaper. Yes. All of that. I let them take care of me. They read me stories, even stories from the newspaper. I don't want to hear those stories. See, Dick. See, Jane. Here comes Spot. Watch Spot run. Here, Spot. Here. Here. In the heart of the city. New York City. And suddenly, it's February. I can begin to walk again—with my nanny. It is still cold outside. I am all bundled up. She takes me to the UN building. She reads to me. The Institute for Training and Research—serving the nations of the world from the UN Headquarters Building in the UN Plaza. I don't understand. Research. What is that? Research about what? Training for what? She doesn't understand either. She pats me on the head. It's OK if you don't understand, she tells me. What is unclear today will be clear tomorrow. But who will teach me? I want to understand. I want to understand it all.

MARCH 14, 1969

Dear Samuel,

The winter is beginning to lose its grip. We are back at the UN building. More stamps. Pretty stamps. One says the Economic Commission for Latin American Facilities in Santiago, Chile. A nice-looking building. A spiral-like building like the building I saw near the Park with the funny name. They told me it was a museum. A place where they have pretty pictures. I'm not sure what they do in the building in Chile. Maybe you can tell me.

May 30, 1969

Dear Samuel,

Springtime in Chicago. I drove here. Alone. Getting back on my feet. On my wheels, as it were. Another American flag stamp. It seems that they put out a new one every year. The stamp is plain enough. Two children pledging allegiance to the flag of the U.S. with their hands over their hearts. I pledge allegiance to the flag of the United States of America. That's as far as it goes. I learned the words when I was in elementary school. I really didn't understand what the words meant. Nobody bothered to explain. Just as long as all of the words were there and pronounced clearly enough—one nation, under God, indivisible. I had problems with that word. Just to pronounce it. Later on, thinking about it. Indivisible as in no effort to secede from the Union—or in defying Federal law. And that phrase—Justice for all. What did that mean in Birmingham? I'm still not clear on what it means to pledge allegiance. Maybe the George Wallaces and Orval Faubuses of the world can help me out on this.

It's good to get out and see the country again. I took all back roads en route. I passed through dozens of small towns in Pennsylvania, Ohio, and Indiana. I had a good feeling doing this. I stopped at every historical marker and visited every historical or natural site I happened to encounter. I sold just enough carpets to keep afloat. No sex toys until I got to Chicago. I'm not sure why. I'm sure there's at least one adult shop in every town above a certain size. I just didn't feel like finding them. I'll be heading back to NYC using main roads now. My friend is waiting for me. I spoke to her on the phone yesterday. She seemed genuinely concerned about my welfare.

June 5, 1969

Dear Samuel,

Back in NYC. Back at the UN. They are celebrating the 50th anniversary of the International Labor Organization—under the heading of labor and development. The stamp shows two workers pushing a giant cogwheel up a ramp. It reminded me of a picture I saw once of the myth of Sisyphus. One of the Titans. The Titans were always getting into trouble with the gods. Atlas was punished by having to bear the weight of the world on his shoulders. Prometheus was chained to a rock and had his liver eaten out by an eagle every day. Tantalus was chained in a pond in such a way that the water and some food were always just out of reach. And Sisyphus was made to roll a rock up a hill. He never had the strength to roll it to the top. When his strength would give out, the stone would roll back down the hill, and he'd have to start all over again. So maybe it's the same with these workers. Modern industry. Does it offer people meaningful, dignified labor at a decent wage, or is it dehumanizing? The assembly line. The organization is fifty years old. That sets it back to 1919, before collective bargaining for wages and better working conditions were legal. If the workers called a strike, Federal troops would be called out to suppress the demonstrators—the same way State Troopers were called out to suppress the marchers in Selma and Birmingham. I guess things are better now for at least some industrial workers. So, selectively, there is something like progress going on. It's just so agonizingly slow and piecemeal. I guess I was never a very patient person. What can I say?

July 16, 1969

Dear Samuel,

San Diego. What a trip! To celebrate California's Bicentennial. I visited the Grand Canyon en route. What a sublime hole in the ground. The stamp emphasizes the Hispanic and Christian roots of the State. But California these days is much more than Hispanic. All those Asians. More ethnic and religious groups than you can shake a stick at. And young people—Hippies and whatnot. Cults. And natural beauty. I got you your stamps and then went North a bit. To the redwood forests. I could spend weeks walking among those trees. I could pitch a tent and live there forever. I have sustenance. Gerber's. The stuff doesn't spoil. It doesn't need cooking. I'm living quite simply these days. I don't need much to keep me going. Not much at all.

November 20, 1969

Dear Samuel,

Meandering. I missed any number of First Day Covers. I can't seem to keep focused on anything for very long. Columbus, Ohio. Fiftieth Anniversary of Easter Seals. Hope for the crippled. Is that a better term than disabled or challenged or something else? Some crippling is mental. You can't see it from the outside. I feel in many ways that I'm just limping through life. There may yet come a time when I'm confined to a wheelchair—metaphorically. I'll sit in a rocking chair in some mental institution and just rock my life away. Hopefully on an outdoor porch so I can hear birds sing and watch squirrels chase each other around.

What is going on in the world? Some industries finally getting behind a consensus on race with regard to hiring and promotions. Wow!

Some sponsors pull out of a golf tournament because it was to be played at a Country Club that excluded minorities from membership. So the Club took in one black member. One of the haves. And he didn't even play golf.

Democrats in South Carolina still refuse to nominate Black candidates. So the Blacks joined together to form a United Citizens Party. Purely symbolic.

Harvard forms a W. E. B. Du Bois Institute for African and Afro-American research. Harvard. Wow! Du Bois was the first Black to earn a PhD from Harvard back in 1899. I read about it. His dissertation was on the Black community in Philadelphia. Then he wrote a book called *The Souls of Black Folk*. I read it a long time ago. Pretty impressive for the time. He was one of the founding members of the NAACP—spearheaded drives for voting and political rights. So I guess naming an Institute after him was appropriate. You often wonder when you see a name on something what the person actually did to merit it. Besides give money. Then again, if you gave enough money, you'd be entitled to some kind of recognition.

Formation of a Black Caucus in Congress. Are there enough Black Senators and Representatives to caucus? Maybe so.

I missed the Christmas stamp. I'm getting unreliable these days. Maybe you should just go with dealers. I can't trust myself to go from point A to point B. Half the time I find myself asking why I'm going here or there. Even if I get to where I think I should be going, more often than not I forget what I was supposed to do. Almost December. The year ending fast. Have I done anything worthwhile in 1969? Anything to justify my existence—my taking oxygen out of the air that some other creature could have used more purposively.

Columbus, Ohio. Not much to do here. Even possibly in NYC. But there are people that know me. Well, and Adam knew his wife. Wife. Friend. I will not be . . . alone.

March 13, 1970

Dear Samuel,

How long has it been? Over three months. I don't want you to worry about me. It takes some effort for me to write these days. To go even to accustomed places. The UN building. How many times have I been there? I go again. Strange stamp. The Lower Mekong Delta Development Program—to make the river more navigable. The same day, another stamp—did I see that before? The Japanese Peace Bell. Maybe they're running out of things to commemorate. Hardly likely. When the Japanese occupied the Mekong Delta, they didn't seem to be thinking about peace. The traditional religion of Japan was supposed to hold that all Japanese were descended from the gods and all non-Japanese were made of inferior stuff—so you don't have to treat them as complete human beings. Convenient. Maybe as only 3/5 human. Where have I heard that before?

I've been having dreams. More like nightmares. I am at my friend's house. She is pampering me. I don't mind. In the dream she is spoon-feeding me some Gerber's dessert—Blueberry Buckle—when my father walks in. He gets a disgusted look on his face. Look at you there, he says. No real man would behave like that. If I had known how you would turn out, I would never have slept with your mother that night. She was a real woman. She knew how to satisfy a man. And to think that the two of us could have produced a wimp like you. A pervert. And it cost her her life. It would have been better had you never been born. She would still be alive. And then he stomps out of the room. The dessert turns bitter in my mouth.

Don't let him get to you, my friend says. You're worth ten of him.

But it doesn't feel that way to me. His words cut into me like a knife. I feel like I am bleeding inside. I am growing weak. I can feel the life draining out of me. I wake up from the dream. It doesn't feel like a dream. I am weak. My energy has been drained from my body. My friend rocks me in her arms. She caresses my hair. I allow myself to calm down. But I fight off sleep as long as I can. Because the nightmares return. Always the same.

MAY 6, 1970

Dear Samuel,

Dinosaurs. The Age of Reptiles. How nice. A big stamp. Brontosaurus, Stegosaurus. Favorite creatures from my childhood. I got every dinosaur book I could find. The names were like magic, rolling off my tongue. Tyrannosaurus Rex, the king of the thunder lizards. Allosaurus. Plesiosaurus. I wanted to be a paleontologist. I wanted to dig up fossils—to discover new creatures from ages past. Maybe even get to name a creature. What would I call it? I'd dream about the name. About going to a museum and seeing a new exhibit of the creature I had discovered. I would run through names to anyone who would listen. My father was not impressed. He thought I was wasting my time on such nonsense. Who cared about creatures that had died millions of years ago? The only thing animals were good for was to be hunted down and killed for meat. Or hunted down for the sheer joy of bagging them—maybe stuffing their heads to hang on the wall. And he did have the head of a 16-point buck on the wall. He was really proud of it. Me, I was a poor fish. No real son of his. Not Richard's son. No indeed.

The envelope shows a ceremonial canoe (the only good Injun is a dead Injun). An American bald eagle (kill the sucker). An African elephant. It takes a real man to bring one of those down. Not the likes of you. If dinosaurs were still alive, I'm sure my Father would have gone after them. It's in the genes, I suppose. Maybe I got her genes, not his. Probably fortunate. I couldn't watch myself burn crosses in someone's front yard—or dragging some Black man to a lynching in front of cheering crowds of grandparents and kindergarteners.

June 26, 1970

Dear Samuel,

Still in NYC. The UN touts its 25th anniversary under the motto "Peace is Progress." What could be wrong with that? One envelope shows a statue symbolizing peace—a gift of the Czechoslovakian government. I guess that should be significant. In the Second World War, different ethnic groups spent their time killing each other—Serbs vs. Croatians, as I recall. The Croatians sided with the Germans. The Serbians fought the Germans. By the end of the war, they managed to kill over a million of each other without any German help. Amazing that they could join together in one Union. Kind of makes our Civil War a small spat by comparison. I read about one incident. The partisans at that point were winning against the pro-fascist forces. The fascists tried to escape across the border but were repulsed by some Allied forces. They returned, only to be captured by the partisans, who shoved them into cattle cars, took them to a deserted place in the woods, and executed them all—about 75,000 of them. No love lost there. Again, it's been less than 30 years. And these people have long memories. They still talk about a battle with the Turks they fought 600 years ago. Like Southerners still talk about the War of Northern Aggression. The South will rise again. The South did rise again at the end of Reconstruction. They got all the wrong lessons—drew all the wrong conclusions. No more slavery. Viva the Klan. As long as you have Black people to suppress, you don't have to face any of your other problems. Our problems.

The other envelope remembers the signing of the UN Charter in San Francisco. I suppose that's something to celebrate. The League of Nations didn't last that long. Then again, we refused to join it—give up one iota of sovereignty to a group of "ferriners." We did join the UN, not that it makes that much difference. We fought in Korea. We're fighting in Viet Nam. So much for international efforts to promote peace.

July 9, 1970

Dear Samuel,

Portland, Maine. The 150th anniversary of Statehood. The stamp shows a lighthouse in Portland Head that was authorized by George Washington. I like Maine. Rugged. Sparsely populated. Look at a map. More than half the state is wilderness. No major roads. The Native Americans want it back. They have a good case. It's not as if they would be displacing a bunch of Whites in the process. Maybe a few lumber companies. That could be significant. In a battle between justice and corporate profits, you know who generally wins. And it would set a precedent—acknowledging past grievances. What next? Give 1/3 of Alabama, Mississippi, et al. back to the Indians. A chunk of the Dakotas back to the Dakotas. Let the Cherokee march back to Tennessee. All those places with Indian names that are now Indian-free, because we chased them out, exiled them, or massacred them. Can't come right out and confess that we were wrong and want to redress the ills—to make it all good again. Reparation. We don't even want to recognize that we were wrong. And if the Indians, what next? The Blacks, the Chinese that were forced to build the railroads out West, the shanty Irish. There's no end to it. The Mexicans. Are we about to return the lands we seized? Most of Arizona and New Mexico. California. Let the Japanese return land they took from the Ainu? Let Australia give back land to the aborigines and New Zealand give back land to the Maori. Where would you stop in your search for justice? Where do you even begin? Maine. Still virgin territory. We are in no real hurry. Just want a few more centuries for the dust to settle.

July 20, 1970

Dear Samuel,

On the road again. Maine to South Dakota to celebrate Wildlife Conservation. The American Bison brought back from near extinction by a cooperative effort of the U.S. and Canada. Poor bison. Killed off in en masse as a way of depriving native Americans of their major food source. Shoot a whole animal for its tongue. Let the carcasses rot in the sun. OK, we don't do that anymore. There are now established herds of bison roaming around the Dakotas. Not too many Dakotas roaming free. We could solve the buffalo issue. People are another matter. Save the animals. The people be damned. Custer, South Dakota. Custer's Last Stand. Wounded Knee. A lot of history here. Better to focus on the buffalo.

AUGUST 6, 1970

Dear Samuel,

I'm back in DC. The stamp commemorates Eisenhower—General, Commander of the troops in Europe during the War, 34th President. I like Ike. That was the slogan. You couldn't say I like Adlai. It didn't flow. Too much of an intellectual anyway. Too liberal. Very few people didn't like Ike. Which was a good thing—to have a President like that. Unite the country. Although he didn't have a Southern strategy—to kowtow to the rednecks. And how can you hate a guy like that, even if he doesn't kiss up to segregationists—and sends Federal troops to integrate the schools in Little Rock?

AUGUST 22, 1970

Dear Samuel,

Petersburg, Illinois. I'm a bit antsy these days. I feel that I have to keep moving.

The stamp honors Edgar Lee Masters (1864–1950), American poet. That's nice. Don't remember too many other poets that have been honored. He published an anthology of other poets' works that was very influential. Which other poets achieved national significance? Whitman. I used to like reading the poetry of Emily Dickinson. Carl Sandburg Jr. T. S. Eliot (oh, he went British). Maybe some of the Harlem Renaissance poets like Langston Hughes—down-to-earth stuff. Simple enough for a child to understand. Maybe Robert Frost. A lot to choose from. Then again, we wouldn't want to make too much of poets. You wouldn't want to let your daughter marry one of them. Hey, Mom. Hey, Dad. I want you to meet my fiancé. What does he do for a living? He writes poetry. Think again. Well, you didn't approve of me going out with a jazz musician. How about . . . a carpenter?

September 12, 1970

Dear Samuel,

Charleston. I hesitated initially. Do I dare? The 300th anniversary of the English settlement in South Carolina—a land grant by Charles II of England. I kind of like that. The King of England granting land to English settlers in the New World. The Indians who had lived there for centuries were not taken into account. And if you don't accept the fact that Indians have any rights, it's only one stop to thinking Blacks have no rights. Where do we go from there?

South Carolina and Georgia were special. England wanted to settle these territories. So they shipped out a group of convicts the way they did in Australia and South Africa. Give people a choice. Be hanged or emigrate. Some of the best families in Georgia and South Carolina trace back to sheep rustlers, pickpockets, and prostitutes. Obviously better stock than Indians and Blacks. Any white is superior to anyone of color. If it's part of God's plan in the Bible, who are we to go against the will of the Divine?

October 17, 1970

Dear Samuel,

Can't keep still. I didn't stay too long in South Carolina—Charleston. The image of the genteel South. The spot where Denmark Vesey led his slave rebellion. And after 1820, it would take an act of the state legislature to free a slave. I slipped into Charleston, and soon thereafter I slipped out again. Headed North and West. Minnesota. Fort Spelling. The 150th anniversary of the Fort, which played a major role in opening up the Northwest to European settlers. Manifest Destiny. From sea to shining sea. Everywhere I go, history weighs on me. I can't just look at trees and mountains and enjoy the view. There is always a story that was played out involving blood. Always . . . something.

November 5, 1970

Dear Samuel,

DC. The new Christmas stamp. I got you the nonreligious one this time. A toy train. Toys in the Attic. And that's the true meaning of Christmas, isn't it? Toys, toys, and more toys. Buy, or your children will think you don't love them anymore. Can't have that. Buy. Support the American economy. I have no children to buy for. How un-American. A stranger in a strange land. I have to get back to NYC. My friend is there.

November 20, 1970

Dear Samuel,

The U.S. Postal Service celebrates the 25th anniversary of the UN. I know a lot of people that think the U.S. should get out of the UN. They resent the idea that we are the principal contributor. They would like to cut out all foreign aid—crawl into our shell and pretend that the rest of the world isn't there. In a sense, that's what I've been doing of late—retreating into my shell. The rest of the world disappears. I become a child again. A young child. A baby. What does a baby know about history or current events? About politics? As long as he is well fed, cleaned, changed, and loved—cuddled, massaged. My friend has accepted that role. Maybe I've become the child I always wanted to be. I have a nanny that dotes over me. What more could I ask for? Yet even that cloys from time to time. An act. A pretense. Methinks the lady doth protest too much. The more I tell myself that this is exactly what I want, the more it gets on my nerves. I want out. Anywhere. Yet I have the feeling that I will return. This has become the very center of my world. This city. This woman. This room.

A quick swing North. Plymouth, Mass. The Mayflower landed here 350 years ago. The stamp shows people praying on the shore. They had a hard winter ahead. They would have starved had it not been for the help of Indians. I wonder. If they had to do it all over again.

There will be two stamps issued on 11/24, one in Montgomery and one in Cincinnati, both commemorating Disabled American Veterans. It's not clear why these two cities were chosen. I have not been back to Alabama for so long. I don't know. I just don't know.

JANUARY 19, 1971

Dear Samuel,

I didn't go either to Montgomery or Cincinnati. I stayed at my friend's place. I haven't left since. For Christmas. For New Year. She takes care of me. She feeds me. She brings me toys to play with. She bathes me. She changes me. It has come to that. She cleans me up when I soil myself.

My favorite toys are puzzles. Jigsaw puzzles. She buys them for me. They are so pretty. She got me a puzzle of some pretty houses in Charleston. I started working on the edges. That's how you do puzzles. You get the edges finished first. Then you fill in the inside. Sometimes you work on one area—one house. Then you fit it into the frame. This puzzle is very hard. It has 500 pieces. It took me two weeks to finish it. Sometimes I wouldn't find the right piece to put into place. Then I would get very angry. Or I would sulk for a while. My friend would find the piece then and fit it in. That was OK. The puzzle was so very hard. I needed a little help to finish it. My friend said the next puzzle wouldn't be so hard. When I finished the puzzle, I wanted to keep it just the way it was. But my friend said there was no room for puzzles in the apartment. I could look at the puzzle for a while, and then we would have to put it back in the box. She would get me an easier puzzle. She bought me a puzzle of a clown in the circus. It was easier. The pieces were bigger. Only 300 pieces. Three hundred and twenty-five pieces, she said. The clown's face was very big. He was smiling. He had a big red nose. He had a big red smile and long red hair. It was a happy picture. I worked on the picture during Christmas. I did the edges first and then filled the puzzle in. It was easier this time. I didn't need much help. Only three or four times. And my friend helped me. She did. I finished the picture before New Year's Day. I looked at the clown for a few minutes. Then I had to take the puzzle apart and put it back into the box. I took every piece apart. I did. Then my friend said it was time to celebrate the New Year. I watched TV. The ball came down over Times Square. People were shouting.

They were cheering. It was the New Year. 1971. I watched TV on New Year's Day. I watched the parade from Pasadena. I watched the parade from Philadelphia. Some of the marchers in Philadelphia looked like the clown in my puzzle. I watched football. One of the teams that played was from Alabama. The Crimson Tide. Not the Red Tide. The Red Tide is made up of little creatures that sting. They kill all the fish. So this was not the Red Tide. No. Not at all. When New Year's was over, I got a new puzzle. And a special dessert. Blueberry Buckle. It comes in a glass jar like all the other food I eat. It is very sweet, like pie without the crust. I got up the next morning. My friend cleaned me up. She gave me a bath. She gave me breakfast. I wore a bib so I wouldn't get my clothes dirty. Then she gave me the new puzzle. Three hundred pieces. She said I would have to do this puzzle all by myself. It was hard. But I did it. All by myself. It was a picture of a farm. There were all kinds of animals on the farm. There were cows and chickens and ducks and geese and pigs. And there were sheep. My friend said that was nice. She showed me a picture of a new stamp that was coming out in Las Vegas. Las Vegas is in Nevada. She showed me on a map. The stamp would have a sheep on it. A mamma sheep and a baby sheep. A baby sheep is called a lamb. A sheep goes baa. The baby sheep is taking food from its mother. That's what baby sheep do. The mother makes milk, and the baby sheep drinks the milk. When it gets bigger, it starts to eat grass. My friend said the stamp celebrates the 450th anniversary of introducing sheep to North America. A long time ago, there were no sheep here. People brought them here a long time ago. They would milk the sheep and make cheese from the milk. That's how you make cheese. From the milk. They would cut the sheep's wool off and use it to make clothes and blankets. Sometimes they would kill the sheep and eat the meat. Sometimes they would even kill the baby sheep for their meat. That is not so very nice. But my friend says that lamb meat is very good. She said she could cook some lamb for me if I wanted. But I just wanted to eat the food from the jars. She said she could get me food in jars that had lamb in it, but I didn't want that. So she didn't buy it for me. She gets me jars with chicken meat in it. That was OK. She said I had to eat some meat, because meat had protein in it, and you needed protein to stay healthy and not get sick. My friend is very smart. She takes good care of me. And she brings me puzzles. I do them all by myself.

March 12, 1971

Dear Samuel,

We go for a walk today. It is still cold out. But not so cold. Soon it will be Spring again. The leaves will open on the trees. And there will be flowers everywhere. We go to the Post Office. My friend tells me there is a special stamp coming out and that I should use the stamp to send you a letter. I will write the letter first, and then we will go to the Post Office and put the special stamp on it. It is a fancy envelope you can only get the first day they sell the stamp. I remember that you like those special envelopes. This one is about people who give blood If people get very sick. They may need an operation. Or they may get into an accident and get all smashed up. They can bleed. A lot. And then they need blood, or they will die. So people give some of their own blood so that other people won't have to die. That is very nice. The envelope shows a person lying down in a bed so they can take the blood. It doesn't hurt. It is nice to do nice things for other people. You feel good when you do nice things for other people. My friend said she felt good taking me to the Post Office. She smiled when she took me there. She knew I would be happy mailing you this letter. I do not write too many letters anymore. I do not know what to write about. All that I do is put together my puzzles. I am getting very good at putting all the pieces together. It's fun watching the picture grow out of the pieces I put together. I like to do this very much. I do. My friend said that she would start buying puzzles with more pieces. She says that I am ready to do a puzzle with 500 pieces. Five hundred pieces. That's what the box says. I count them to make sure. There are exactly 500 pieces in the puzzle. I count them again just to make sure.

May 7, 1971

Dear Samuel,

My friend showed me a newspaper. It said that the Supreme Court upheld the desegregation of schools using the busing of students to achieve integration. I didn't understand. She explained everything to me. Some people wanted to keep White children and Black children from going to school together. So they put the schools in areas where only white children and only black children lived. Some other people thought it was a good idea for white children and black children to learn together. So they started busing children from one neighborhood to another so all children could learn together. And the Court said that was OK, because the schools in black neighborhoods weren't as good as the schools in the White neighborhoods, and this way, all the children could get the same education. But that didn't work out, because some of the parents of the white children took their children out of public schools and sent them to private schools that had only white children in them. That's what my friend told me. I didn't understand everything she said. I'm not sure why people do what they do. But I am explaining everything the best that I can. Maybe you will understand

They are having a special stamp to remember the first airmail that happened in our country sixty years ago not far away, in Long Island. I guess that before, they had to send letters like this by train, and it took a very long time to get there. I think they will send this letter to you on an airplane. That way it will get to you really fast. They are going to celebrate in Spokane, Washington. That is very far away—all the way across the country. My friend said it is more than 3,000 miles away. So we didn't go there for the celebration. I remember . . . I think it was in Washington a long time ago. There was a beautiful mountain there with snow on top, even though it wasn't winter. One day maybe I will see that mountain again. One day, maybe soon.

May 8, 1971

Dear Samuel,

I am writing to you again. They are having another celebration. It is only halfway across the country—in Missouri. My friend showed me on the map. The state of Missouri is 150 years old. She showed me a big arch they built in St. Louis. They called the arch the Gateway to the West. That is, if you are going West. I think that if you are coming from the West, you could call it the Gateway to the East. My friend said you could take a spiral elevator to the top of the arch and look out and see things that were far away. She said she did that once, and there was nothing much to see. If you looked to the East, all you could see was East St. Louis, which was a very poor town. Way back in 1919, the Black soldiers came back from fighting in World War I—to make the world safe for democracy. The soldiers wanted to be treated the same as Whites. The Whites started a big riot, and many people were hurt. Some were killed. So if you knew all that happened in East St. Louis, maybe you would want to look at it from the top of the arch. The stamp shows people going out West in covered wagons. They would put everything they had in the wagons—the children too. The men would ride on horses. They would go West to start a new life. Some of them settled in Missouri. My friend said there were fights back then to see if the people in Missouri would have slaves or not. There were bad fights in Missouri and Kansas. Then they figured out which states would have slaves and which couldn't. She said that was called the Missouri Compromise. She told me a lot of things about that. I don't remember them too clearly. I don't always understand what she tells me. I don't understand a lot these days. All I do is work on my puzzles. I am getting very good at puzzles. I can put all the pieces together in less than a week.

MAY 11, 1971

Dear Samuel,

There is a stamp coming out in Washington DC. I have been there many times. The stamp has a picture of the White House on it. That is where the President lives. The President now is Richard Nixon. Richard Milhous Nixon. My friend doesn't like the President. I don't like him either. His name is Richard, just like my father. I really shouldn't dislike the President just because of his name. But every time I think of him, I think about my father. I still dream about my father watching me and spitting tobacco juice on the floor. I don't think the President would spit tobacco juice on the floor. The first President to live in the White House was the second President of the U.S.—John Adams. The White House is a very beautiful place. My friend said that the British burned it during the War of 1812. That was a very mean thing to do. But the British lost the war. I guess they rebuilt the White House after that. And all of the Presidents live there with their wives and children. Even President Nixon, whose first name is my father's name. I guess he didn't choose that name. They gave it to him when he was born. There's a lot of things we get stuck with when we get born. If you have a name like that, I guess you have to live with it whether you like it or not.

June 23, 1971

Dear Samuel,

Another stamp from Washington DC—celebrating the 10th anniversary of the Antarctic Treaty. My friend explained it all to me. Everywhere else in the world if a country sent explorers someplace, they would say that the new land belonged to the country they came from. Even if there were other people living in the country before. They did this in Asia and Africa, in North and South America. Some of these countries have now become free. They belong to the people who live there, not to another country far away. Ten years ago, all the countries in the world decided not to do the same thing at the South Pole. The land would not belong to only one country. It would belong to everybody in the world.

I don't know why anyone would want to have this land. It is so cold. And nobody lives there. Just penguins. I don't know why countries would fight for a land, just to own a bunch of penguins. But my friend says they are doing scientific research down there. They are building research facilities. So scientists can study whatever scientists study. Scientists from all over the world, not just from one country. That way, everybody can learn from whatever anybody finds out. So I guess that is good. My friend showed me Antarctic on a globe. It looks like it does on the stamp. The Antarctic is white because it is always covered with snow and ice. The ocean around it is blue. Deep blue. My friend says that seawater is bluish-green, but blue is OK. You know it's water, even if the color isn't exactly the same.

My friend showed me something in the newspaper. There was a radio station that thought that all black people and all white people should be separate from each other. It kept saying that every day. The government thought that was a bad idea and took the station's license away and let the station be run by people who thought black people and white people should be together. She tried to explain to me how you could do that—to balance Freedom of Speech and . . . something else. I don't remember. But then there was a fight between people who thought it was OK for local stations to say whatever they wanted without the government saying they couldn't and those that said the government had the right to stop stations from saying really bad things. My friend talked about this for a really long time. I kept working on my puzzle.

July 1, 1971

Dear Samuel,

My friend told me the next new stamp would come out in Birmingham. I started to cry. I have not been to Birmingham for so long. I made her get me a book with pictures of Birmingham. I remembered the places they showed in the pictures. I told her I wanted to go home. I really did. She said she would think about it. Maybe she would talk to you about making arrangements. She wanted to make sure that that's what I wanted. I said I was sure. She said she would find me a puzzle I could work on that was a picture of Birmingham. I said that would be nice. It was a big puzzle. A thousand pieces. That would be very hard. With very small pieces. She said that by the time I finished it, she would have an answer for me. So I started working on the puzzle. I worked very hard. The puzzle was very hard. I got the edges finished, but sometimes I would work all day and only find a few pieces to fit in. She told me to have patience. The more I did, the easier it would become. So I kept working on the puzzle. I didn't know how long it would take me to finish it. But I will finish it. And then I will know.

August 2, 1971

Dear Samuel,

I have been working on the puzzle for a month. My friend said there was a new stamp coming out to honor an American painter—John Sloan. He did paintings and etchings. He died 20 years ago. My friend said the stamp would come out in Lock Haven, Pennsylvania. She showed me on the map where it was. Pennsylvania is not so far from New York. But I didn't want to go to Pennsylvania. I want to work on my puzzle. I am filling in some of the spaces. It is taking me a long time. But it doesn't matter how long it takes. I will finish it. I know I will finish it. And then I will know.

October 4, 1971

Dear Samuel,

I am still working on the puzzle. More than half of it is finished now. My friend showed me a picture of a new stamp that will come out in Dallas, Texas. It is about drug abuse. People use drugs, and then they can't do anything else anymore. The drugs are expensive. They spend all their money to get more. Sometimes they steal from other people to get the money. If they are caught by the police, they are sent to jail. I asked my friend why people would do that. She said that once a person started taking the drugs, it was very hard to stop. I asked her why people would start if they knew this was going to happen. She said she didn't understand that either, but sometimes people just do strange things that don't make sense. I guess if it made sense, there would be no problem understanding why.

I am trying hard to finish my puzzle. That makes sense. Because when I am finished, I will know. My friend promised me that. And she keeps her promises. I will finish the puzzle. And then I will know.

October 23, 1971

Dear Samuel,

My friend took me to the Central Post Office in New York to get a new stamp to send to you. The 25th anniversary of CARE. Care stands for Cooperation for American Relief Everywhere. I didn't understand the name. My friend told me that CARE sends food packages to people around the world who are hungry. They send tools to poor people so they can work. All of that is a good thing. It's nice to care about people who need help. I didn't want to take time out from working on my puzzle, but it is almost finished. And the weather is so nice, she thought I should be getting out—because it will start getting cold soon. I should enjoy the outdoors when it is still nice. She said she would have a surprise for me soon. And that is because she really cares for me. So maybe the stamp was for her too. I am almost finished with the puzzle. I have been working on it for a very long time. It's almost finished. Just a few more days. And then I will know.

October 29, 1971

Dear Samuel,

My friend told me about a new stamp. The Historical Preservation Series. Important things people want to preserve out West—the Cable Cars from San Francisco. The Charles W. Morgan whaling ship. The San Xavier del Bac Mission in Tucson, Arizona. I guess it's a good thing to preserve memories from the past.

But I am more interested in today. I finished the puzzle today. I told my friend I wanted to keep this one whole. I wanted her to keep it as a gift from me. To remember me. Because she said she had worked everything out with you. There is a place that I can stay where they will take care of me. They will give me all the puzzles I want to work on. They will feed me all the food I like. I will be able to see you every day. But you have to promise me that you won't tell my father that I'm there. I don't want him to know. I don't want him to see me ever again.

All my things are packed. Not the carpets. I gave all of them away. Not the toys. I gave them away too. I have a copy of the new stamp and the fancy envelope for you about the things they are preserving out West. But I don't care much about those things. I am interested in Birmingham. Now. It has been a long, long time. But I am going home.

www.ingramcontent.com/pod-product-compliance
Lightning Source LLC
Chambersburg PA
CBHW051649180726
48284CB00006B/1924

* 9 7 8 1 9 5 0 8 1 8 7 2 3 *